T0381501

Conversation and Conversion by the Well

A HANDBOOK FOR DIRECTORS OF THE SAMARITAN WOMAN RETREAT

JUDITH A. RINEK, S.N.J.M.

Waters that are living do not stay contained
in stony wells of our own making:
but rather are far flung by Spirit and
seep deep in Truth to parched places
and unquenchable thirsts.

Judith A. Rinek, SNJM

www.trafford.com

North America & international
toll-free: 844-688-6899 (USA & Canada)
fax: 812 355 4082

Dedication

In honor of Petra Berg, S.N.J.M.,
who through her generous writing of letters,
communicated unconditional love and support.
I will always be grateful for her
deep faith in God,
her way of listening that led to the discovery
of opportunities hidden within challenges,
and her belief in me.

*"I came so that they might have life
and have it to the full."*

John 10:10

Jesus and the Samaritan Woman by Gustave Dorè

The Story Begins

He had to pass through Samaria, and his journey brought him to a Samaritan town named Shechem near the plot of land which Jacob had given to his son Joseph. This was the site of Jacob's well. Jesus, tired from his journey, sat down at the well. The hour was about noon. When a Samaritan woman came to draw water, Jesus said to her, "Give me a drink." (His disciples had gone off to the town to buy provisions.) The Samaritan woman said to him, "You are a Jew. How can you ask me, a Samaritan and a woman, for a drink?" (Recall that the Jews have nothing to do with Samaritans). Jesus replied:

"If only you recognized God's gift, and who it is who is asking you for a drink, you would have asked him instead, and he would have given you living water."

"'Sir," she challenged him, "You do not have a bucket and this well is deep. Where do you expect to get this flowing water? Surely you do not pretend to be greater than our ancestor Jacob, who gave us this well and drank from it with his sons and his flocks?" Jesus replied:

"Everyone who drinks this water will be thirsty again. But whoever drinks the water I give will never be thirsty; no, the water I give shall become a fountain within, leaping up to provide eternal life."

The woman said to him, "Give me this water, Sir, so that I shall not grow thirsty and have to keep coming here to draw water."

John 4:4–16, Translation from New American Bible, P.J. Kennedy & Sons, 1970

Contents

Acknowledgements

If the Holy Spirit had not inspired the creator of the Samaritan Woman Directed Retreat, Almita Bey-Carrión, if the people had not come seeking the "living waters," if directors had not been willing to guide them there, this handbook would not have come to be. In writing the handbook for directors of this transforming experience, I am most grateful for the collaboration of many dedicated people.

❖ Most deeply, I appreciate the men and women who welcomed me into the journey of their lives so that this specialized form of spiritual direction could move them forward. They have challenged me, delighted me, and revealed the depths and richness of this Gospel story. May God's blessing be upon them as they continue to live the deepest desires of their heart with greater integrity.

❖ I would not have known the power and the possibilities of this retreat if I had not experienced it for myself. Thus, I am ever grateful to Almita Bey-Carrión for taking me there at a crossroads in my own life. As the retreat has evolved over the years from her initial creation, she has continued to offer her insights and suggestions for editing it.

❖ In making this handbook as useful as possible for directors, the involvement of other spiritual directors has been especially important. Rev. Marilyn Omernick updated the theology and language in the meditations; Linda Marie Amador and Sandra Linderman spent many hours selecting passages from Almita's original thesis, critiquing the materials for the provisional handbook and writing sections that help directors prepare well for the directee and help directees utilize the meditations more effectively. Linda also designed an attractive brochure inviting others to the "living waters."

❖ Sr. Thomas Bernard, C.S.J., Linda Flynn, Sr. Laura Gormley, S.S.L., Kay Murdy, Fr. Al Pooler, C.P., Sr. Carol Reis, S.N.J.M., Sr. Barbara Williams, S.N.J.M., Flora Slosson Wuellner, and other spiritual directors have offered helpful suggestions along the way. I am grateful for their enthusiasm and support for this handbook.

❖ Only when I plunged into the process of publishing these materials did I realize that other resources were essential: the Sisters of the Holy Names of Jesus and Mary gave me a mini-grant to publish a professional handbook; my place of ministry, Mater Dolorosa Passionist Retreat Center in Sierra Madre, California, promoted and supported this customized retreat and the training of spiritual directors who lead it; Jan Johnson edited materials written over a ten-year period and shaped them into one coherent document; Maura and Steve Walsh provided the technology needed for on-demand digital publishing; and Susan Rinek added her graphic design expertise to the format and the cover design.

Because of the dynamic and creative energy of the Holy Spirit, many in the future will lend their experience and suggestion to enhance this retreat and this handbook. It is now out of Almita's hands, out of mine, and into yours. I gratefully acknowledge all of you.

Sr. Judy Rinek, S.N.J.M.
Mater Dolorosa Passionist Retreat Center
Sierra Madre, California
Pentecost
May 15, 2005

Foreword

By Almita Bey-Carrión

The day Sister Judy Rinek came into my life, thirteen years ago now, ushered in a rich, joy-filled source of blessings, inspiration, and lasting friendship. We met on a women's retreat at Mater Dolorosa Passionist Retreat Center in Sierra Madre, California. Judy was attending the retreat, and I, at that time, was a member of the retreat team along with three Passionist priests and a Passionist brother. I was immediately drawn to Judy's outgoing, warm personality. In getting to know one another we discovered mutual areas of interest. High on the list was a love of spirituality, the outdoors, and hiking. We soon became friends and hiking buddies and have remained so to this day.

What I appreciate most about Judy, apart from our times of fun and laughter, is our ability to have in-depth conversations, yet we are comfortable sharing times of silence. Perhaps these latter qualities are part of what drew her to the Samaritan Woman Directed Retreat because it invites the directee to an in-depth conversation with Jesus, while at the same time listening in silence to his of her deepest conflicts, weaknesses, and issues. This dynamic of listening followed by silent reflection leads to the truth and healing Jesus wants to bring.

Judy was curious and interested in the retreat from when I first explained it to her. A couple of years later she asked if I would be her spiritual director for this retreat, to which I agreed. I had moved to southern Nevada by then, so she arranged to come to my home for ten days. Typical of anything Judy commits to, she gave her all to the retreat and emerged with new insights about herself and a deepened relationship with Jesus. Yet something else happened: Judy now had a vision and conviction that here was something powerful and life-changing that needed to be shared. Her determination to see this retreat made available to others put her on a path neither she nor I could have anticipated. She began directing the retreat herself, and from there other spiritual directors, having made the retreat with her, went on to become directors of the retreat. Judy put together special information evenings regarding the Samaritan Woman Directed Retreat that resulted in several people becoming interested and eventually making the retreat with her or with one of the other available directors.

My husband and I moved to Nevada in 1994. Once here, my ministry of spiritual direction that I had been such a big part of my life for twenty years, more or less phased out. Furthermore, I had not directed the Samaritan Woman Directed Retreat for several years and felt a growing distance between the retreat and my competency to direct it. It was Sr. Judy who was keeping it "alive and well." Not only that, I saw that she had a broader and better-informed understanding of its dynamics and the various disciplines from which it drew. She creatively embellished each meditation with visuals, handouts, and in some cases, suggested activities. With the help of others she revised the language of the retreat to be more inclusive and, thus, appeal to a broader audience. Sr. Judy Rinek had become the true champion of the Samaritan Woman Directed Retreat. With her own divine inspiration and untiring energy, she had taken it up where I had left off

In time Judy realized that a handbook for directors of the retreat was needed. As with everything she does, Judy approached this project with enthusiasm and drive. She arranged a three-day brain-storming session between she and I and two other directors of the retreat. So it was that on a balmy afternoon, while the four of us sat by the flowing Carson River here in northern Nevada where I now live, that the handbook began to unfold. What you now hold in your hands is the result of much dedication, organization and hard work done primarily by Judy, although others contributions toward the finished product were invaluable. These people are acknowledged in the text.

As the years passed, it became increasingly clear to me that God had somehow chosen me to bring this retreat into the world, but God had chosen Judy to bring it to full maturity. After a time of prayer and discernment, I made the decision to turn the retreat and its future over to the very capable hands of my dear friend, Sr. Judy, and to the Sisters of the Holy Names of Jesus and Mary, to which she belongs. There is no doubt in my mind that this was God's plan all along. Over the past fifteen years, the Holy Spirit has patiently guided us to fulfill our prescribed and individual roles regarding the Samaritan Woman Directed Retreat.

I want to take this opportunity to thank Sr. Judy for following the promptings of her soul regarding this retreat that came to me during one prayer time long ago. I want to thank her for not allowing this retreat to die on the shelf of my den and for being such a trustworthy guardian of what we and others believe will continue to be a great blessing in the lives of many who complete the *Nine Meditations* that comprise the retreat. Most of all I want to thank her for her unrelenting efforts regarding the dissemination of the Samaritan Woman Directed Retreat, which now includes this valuable handbook for directors which she has successfully and professionally authored.

Judy keeps me informed on the growth and expansion of the retreat. It never ceases to amaze me how consistently affirming the evaluations are by those who complete the *Nine Meditations* of the retreat. This was true from when I was the only one directing it back in the early 1990's. The most repeated comment then and now is that it is a positive, life-changing experience. Clearly, the vitality and blessings of the retreat continue under the guidance of new directors.

"The woman then left her water jar and went off into the town." (John 4:28) Many water jars have and will continue to be left behind as we go back to our lives transformed and inspired by this intimate conversation with Jesus. No longer needing our "well," no longer confined by its imposed and often false limitations, we go forward freed and strengthened by Jesus' gift of "living waters" to become all God created us to be. To Sr. Judy Rinek and to all who feel called to direct this retreat, my prayers and blessings go with you and those whom you bring to the living waters.

Almita Bey-Carrión
Gardnerville, Nevada
April 26, 2005
Easter Season

Almita Bey-Carriòn, the creator of *The Samaritan Woman Directed Retreat*, received her M.A. in spirituality from the University of Santa Clara, California. She has been a spiritual director for over twenty years and was on the Passionist Retreat Team at Mater Dolorosa Retreat Center from 1988-1994. In 1994 she and her husband, Rueben, relocated to Pahrump, Nevada, and moved seven years later to Garnerville in northern Nevada. Almita facilitates a Woman's Scripture Sharing Group and a Contemplative Prayer Group in her parish of St. Gall, where she is also Dean of the Benedictine Oblates. Mother of five grown children, she makes time for her hobbies of bird-watching and photography in, to quote her, "the beauty and grandeur of the Sierra Nevada."

Preface

Purpose

Are you thirsting for the living waters Jesus came to bring? Within this book you will go on a journey with Jesus to find these waters bubbling up within. Besides exploring the story found in John 4 of the Bible as your story, you will find within this book resources to go even further. The spiritual journey is like a spiral, ever deepening.

Originally, this handbook was developed for spiritual directors of the Samaritan Woman Directed Retreat. If that describes you, this handbook will connect you with the origin of the retreat and keep you faithful to the gift of the Spirit given to Almita Bey-Carrión that has been so transforming for people in mid-life. The Samaritan Woman Directed Retreat invites you to follow the lead of the Spirit as you apply your own creativity, resources and giftedness in directing people throughout the retreat. More specifically, within this handbook you will find the meditations composed by Almita (Chapter 3), information on a wide variety of pertinent issues encountered during the retreat (Chapters 4, 5, and 6), background on the dynamics of spiritual direction (Chapter 7), and development of the psychology and spirituality (Chapters 8 and 9) basic to the retreat. These materials serve as a reminder of what you already know and point to additional sources for your own professional growth (Chapters 11 and 12).

Other readers of this handbook may be spiritual directors who have heard about this retreat and want to know more about it. Especially, if you are working with men and women discerning a call to religious life, integrating spirituality with their recovery from addiction, emerging from depression or a life-threatening illness, or wrestling with mid-life issues, this retreat will be a profound experience for them. If that is you, both Almita Bey-Carrión and I emphasize that in order to offer this customized retreat to others, you have to be competent in the ministry of spiritual direction and you have to experience the retreat itself. In order to make this retreat, please, seek out a director who has been trained in this approach. A list of them can be found by consulting the trafford.com webpage or the appendix. Retreat centers such as Mater Dolorosa Passionist Retreat Center in Sierra Madre, California, can accommodate you for a 10-day retreat, if you have to travel a long distance. As more directors become trained, the geographical areas served will expand.

You may be a director of RCIA (Rite for Christian Initiation of Adults) or on a team for RCIA,—that is, a conversion process for adults that leads them to the sacraments of initiation in the Catholic Church. During the final weeks of preparation in Lent, the Samaritan woman story is one of the Sunday Gospels that illustrates growth in faith and discipleship. Chapters 7, 8, and 9 of this handbook provide an in-depth exploration of this story. Spiritual directors for the catechumens would find this individualized retreat as an ideal way to lead them beyond what blocks their conversion and intimate relationship with Jesus. If a group experience is preferred, see the outstanding retreats developed by Sr. Miriam Malone, S.N.J.M. in her book, *Enter the Rose: Retreats for Unfolding the Mysteries of Faith with Catechumens, Candidates and All Believers* (World Library Publications, c. 2004, www.wlpmusic.com).

However, you may be one of those who have already made the retreat. As life unfolds, you will find most of the handbook as a useful reference for processing and integrating your experience. The chapters on Origins (Chapter 2), Spirituality of the Retreat (Chapter 8) and Psychology of the Retreat (Chapter 9) may be especially of interest to you. Moreover, the bibliography (Chapter 12) provides many resources for deepening your spiritual growth.

Permissions for the Materials

To make these materials more accessible to spiritual directors who have already experienced this retreat, Almita Bey-Carrión has given owners of this handbook permission to copy her meditations found in Chapter 3 for each directee making the retreat. To her generous gesture I add my own: you may duplicate the handout, "Preparing For and Working Through the Samaritan Woman Directed Retreat Sessions," in Chapter 3 and appropriate handouts from Chapter 11, without explicit permission. Quotations less than a page may be used in publicity, teaching or writing. If entire chapters are desired by another—for example, Spirituality of this Retreat, Chapter 8—please, have that person purchase a copy of the handbook from the trafford.com webpage.

Honoring the copyright means:

❖ Use these materials under the conditions stated in the handbook

❖ Acknowledge the appropriate authors as the source

Making this Handbook "User-friendly"

Many of the users of this handbook will prefer to keep the contents intact in this spiral bound book. This unique binding allows for a flat open book and facilitates the process of reproducing meditations and resources of this retreat.

Others may prefer to be creative with its contents. You may easily convert this book into a three-ring notebook format by doing the following:

1. Select a 1 ½ inch spine, 11 ½ inch by 10 ½ inch view binder
2. Cut off the spiral coil of this handbook
3. Trim off the side with the holes--front and back covers
4. Trim the side of the pages with the holes; secure each page in a three-hole plastic protector and insert in the notebook. The plastic protector preserves each page from heavy usage and makes possible the use of post-it notes to add your own tips and comments for each page.
5. Blank pages can be added for your own notes and resources for the appropriate sections
6. Now you are ready to begin!

Part I

The Context

1

Introduction: Why Develop a Handbook for
the Samaritan Woman Directed Retreat?

Options at Mid-life

Most of the energy in the first half of life is spent in developing our personality, our career and our relationships. Unconsciously, we formulate a frame of reference we call reality. It includes expectations and concepts of self, others, the world and God. Trauma (such as death of a loved one, emerging memories of abuse, a wrenching divorce or life-threatening illness) is one of the life experiences that shifts this frame of reference. Suddenly, we discover the illusions, assumptions and limitations of our former reality.

We find ourselves isolated from those who still live comfortably within "the box"—that is, this once familiar frame of reference. Our encounter with the truth of life often happens at mid-life and plagues us with unsettling questions, a broader perspective and new choices. Will we opt out of a life that has become too disorienting, depressing, and overwhelming? Suicide and drugs are the unfortunate coping strategies of all too many. Will we try to return to our former reality by repressing our feelings, denying our experience and pretending that all is well? The following tragic story of the tiger Mohini illustrates the rigid and restricted experience of life in that choice. This story is reflected upon by inmate Charles "Tom" Brown from prison in Buckeye, Arizona. His trauma was incarceration. Within that experience he chose a third type of response:

> Mohini, a white tiger, spent years pacing back and forth in her twelve-by-twelve-foot cage in the National Zoo in Washington, D.C. Eventually, a natural habitat was created for her. Covering several acres, it had hills, trees, a pond, and a variety of vegetation. With excitement and anticipation, the staff released Mohini into her new and expansive environment. The tiger immediately sought refuge in the corner of the compound. There she lived for the remainder of her life, pacing back and forth in an area measuring twelve feet by twelve feet.
>
> Some prisons are built with concrete, steel, and razor wire. Others are built in the dungeons of our minds. Though freedom is possible, we often pass our years trapped in the same old patterns. We cage ourselves in to self-imposed prisons with self-judgment and anxiety. Then, with the passing of time, we like Mohini, grow incapable of accessing the freedom and peace that is our birthright.

Life, however, is continually calling us to be more, to journey into the wilderness and face the truth. In my case, the shell of my life had to be softened—broken down, even—by the experience of coming to prison, before the moment of truth could appear. I needed to be humbled, cooked in tears of loss, for any deeper life to emerge.

A new life requires a death of some kind; otherwise, it is nothing new but the shuffling of the same old deck. What dies is an outworn way of being in the world. We are no longer who we thought we were.

On the deepest level, this journey of awakening opens us up to the innermost center of love. Love creates its own freedom from imprisonment, has its own direction, moves according to its own rhythms, and makes it own music.

Ironically, in the experience of prison Tom found freedom, love and truth. His incarceration initiated the second half of his life. After facing the losses and the pain, he discovered a new reality, a more true understanding and response to life. Though he does not use religious language to interpret what happened, he has glimpsed the fullness of life Jesus proclaims in John 10:10: "I came so that they might have life and have it to the full."

Often the second half of life begins in darkness. We feel alone and isolated. The way forward seems to have perilous detours and unfamiliar terrain. Mystics such as John of the Cross call this phase of our spiritual journey "the dark night of the soul." It is but one stage in growth toward intimate union with God. Jungian psychologists speak of this transition as essential to the "individuation process." The goal is the emergence of one's true Self. Both spirituality and psychology bring important resources to this phase of our life.

Spiritual directors who have "been there," are reliable companions for mid-life men and women who are finding their way in the dark. The power of fear and denial is very strong; the unconscious does not yield its treasures too readily. Consequently, the intuition and support of trusted and experienced guides at this point in life are irreplaceable. As this handbook unfolds, you will see how the Samaritan Woman Directed Retreat is an important resource for these guides. Entering this treacherous, mystical journey myself, I could not foresee where it would take me. Here is how a ministry to those in mid-life developed.

Story Behind the Handbook

Since I have made several retreats throughout my life, explored many spiritual traditions, and spent many years in the process of healing of inner wounds, I did not expect anything new to happen. Out of curiosity I had asked Almita Bey-Carrión to guide me in a retreat she had created. The prospect of making it had come up in our conversation regarding her master's thesis for Santa Clara University (Santa Clara, California). To complete her thesis, she was required to guide several people through the retreat. Because she had written so eloquently on how the retreat had transformed their lives, I was surprised that it essentially remained "on the shelf" since 1992.

In October, 1996, I cleared my calendar for ten days at my place of ministry, Mater Dolorosa Passionist Retreat Center in Sierra Madre, California. Then I set off for Almita's home in Pahrump, Nevada, to experience the Samaritan Woman Directed Retreat. My life has never been the same! The surprises and power of the Holy Spirit were evident during my retreat and for many years afterwards as I continued to integrate the graces and decisions that flowed from it. As I was pondering how I might share this life-changing experience with others, I made a pilgrimage to the places significant to the origins of my religious community in Canada. As I walked into the motherhouse chapel in Montreal, I was immediately struck by the large mosaic in the dome above the altar. Beneath the figures of Jesus, Mary and the saints was a shelf of rock. Out of the rock gushed many streams of water. The abundance and vitality of those waters reminded me of the promise of "living water" made by Jesus to the Samaritan Woman. This mosaic in the motherhouse seemed to confirm for me an intuition that it would be the Sisters of the Holy Names who would bring this gift to many. I was convinced that it was time to take this retreat "off the shelf" so that many others could experience this direct encounter with Jesus. With Almita's encouragement I did just that.

Over the past ten years I have directed over thirty people through this retreat. As word got out, some of the interested people had to wait for an opening several months away. Subsequently, I discovered a few other spiritual directors, who having made the retreat, felt drawn to facilitate this experience. Out of our shared ministry came a need for a handbook. As Almita reflected in her e-mail, January 18, 2004: "… I do believe in the importance of the handbook and in the vitality and gift of the retreat itself. At times I have to remind myself that it all started with the inspiration God chose to give me during a difficult period of my life. It's only when I recall my own fervor as former director of this retreat along with my belief that it is meant to be part of our church's rich store of spiritual offerings, that I can feel that fire again. It's true that if it weren't for your long-standing belief and excitement over this retreat, it would have died with me. As I've expressed to you before, Judy, I may have been the author God chose for this retreat, but you are the one God calls to carry it into the world as well as motivate others to do the same."

Many of the readers of this handbook share the same excitement about this retreat. Having made the retreat yourself, you as a director know much about the elements, flow, and purpose of the Samaritan Woman Directed Retreat. Leading others through it will both confirm your own experience and open up new possibilities for you. Each person you guide will amaze you. How differently each responds to the same meditations! Throughout the retreat, the directees seem to find what they most need at this stage of their spiritual journey. Many who make this retreat speak of it helping them "to come home," as if most of their life had been lived in "exile."

Overview of the Retreat

Like a hologram, the Gospel story of the Samaritan woman at the well has much depth and many dimensions. Spiritual directors of these mid-life wanderers will find in the story the dynamics of conversion that facilitates the treacherous passage from the old ways of being into the new. Within Chapters 3, 4, 5 and 6 are the materials for the retreat and practical suggestions on how to prepare oneself as director as well as how to animate this retreat for another.

For those used to the distinctions between "spiritual direction" and "retreat," a clarification may be useful. First of all, this "retreat" created by Almita Bey-Carrión is meant to take place in the context of individual spiritual direction. As such, the experience is neither the classical understanding of spiritual direction nor of retreat. A person does not necessarily attend a retreat center; he or she has no common schedule or group. Yet, the Samaritan Woman Directed Retreat does have designated meditations that one might find in a retreat setting. While providing flexibility so that the Spirit may work through the interaction of the director and directee, the meditations give security and structure for someone just beginning spiritual direction or who feels vulnerable and lost. The success of the retreat also depends upon the listening, sensitivity, and resources of the director who stands with a person at his or her dark well and facilitates an encounter with the healing, caring, freeing and empowering presence of Christ. Since this inner journey occurs in the midst of daily life, this retreat may be considered a specialized form of spiritual direction.

Moreover, the Samaritan Woman Directed Retreat may dovetail with your spiritual direction ministry. For example, you may recognize that one of your directees is struggling with mid-life issues. When the retreat begins, monthly direction would shift into a weekly or every other week mode; the content of your conversation would shift from noticing God in ones' daily life to encountering God in the context of one's whole life—past, present and future. The style of the directee's prayer may change to a more contemplative mode. You will also discover that the discipline of meditation and journal work during this time will give your directee a habit of listening deeply to Jesus' response that will continue to enhance the quality of the spiritual direction experience long after the retreat is over.

Like the 19th Annotation of the Spiritual Exercises of St. Ignatius, the Samaritan Woman Directed Retreat is flexible and customized to the schedule and circumstances of the person making the retreat. Basically, it consists of nine segments taken from John 4:4–42. The process of reflecting on the word of God and on one's life is meant to engage directees in a transforming dialogue with Jesus. Especially if they are stuck in their spiritual growth, experiencing a change, or feeling a sense of something missing in life, this dialogue can help access deeper desires, engage the subtle power of the Holy Spirit, see self from the perspective of God's unconditional love, and release them from all that holds them back from living fully. <u>Thus, this retreat has been most helpful to women and men negotiating mid-life issues, recovering from addictions or life-threatening illnesses, or contemplating a major life changes or decisions.</u>

Four Fonts of Spirituality

The spirituality of this retreat is symbolized by the fountain on the cover of this handbook. *Living water*, as the Hebrews understood it, was water that moved—streams, rivers, gushing springs and fountains. These waters sustained life, were purified and oxygenated as they percolated through layers of earth, splashed over rocks and exposed their surface to the sunlight. Sitting water, especially pools found in deep, dark areas can stagnate. This fountain image adds other dimensions. Like the prisms of rain, the splash of water in a fountain creates a rainbow. A sign of hope and God's covenant with Noah (Gen. 9:12–17), this rainbow is also a metaphor of that hope and deep bonding with God that many experience during this retreat. Moreover, these leaping fonts of water, though many, come from the same source. Jesus calls this source the Spirit.

There are four main fonts of spirituality that sustain this retreat:
1. Biblical—Study, inspiration and conversion
2. Benedictine—*Lectio Divina* approach to meditation
3. Ignatian—Dynamics of the Spiritual Exercises of St. Ignatius, Ignatian contemplation
4. Twelve Step—Spiritual program for release from addiction, compulsion and obsession

The font of psychology that animates this retreat is Jungian. It emphasizes story, symbol, dream work, shadow, archetype of Self and process of individuation. These fonts are supported by:

❖ Journal writing that claims one's experience, prayer and healing
❖ Mandala art that promotes insight, healing, self-expression, balance, harmony and spiritual well-being
❖ Mid-life emphasis that addresses the crossroads in psycho-spiritual development
❖ Spiritual direction that customizes this retreat for the directee

A Word to Spiritual Directors

Collaborating with Almita Bey-Carrión and the other spiritual directors, I have written this handbook with you in mind. Be assured of our prayers for God's blessing each time you invite someone to seek the "living waters."

2

Origins: Where Did this Retreat Come From?

Almita Bey-Carrión recalls how this retreat came to her in her master's thesis, *The Samaritan Woman Directed Retreat* (University of Santa Clara, 1992, updated version, 2005; pp. 1–13):

Personal Encounter

"It was a prayer time like any other. I settled in comfortably to begin my daily ritual of scripture reading, reflection, and journal writing—perhaps to include other reading or private devotions. Looking back now, I realize that a seed was planted that day. The Holy Spirit passed through me dropping a seed of inspiration that in its own time would take root to emerge as spiritual fruit to be shared with others. In this respect, it was not a prayer time like any other.

"That particular day, July, 3, 1990, remains a picture in my memory. I recall so vividly what happened to me as I began to read the fourth chapter in the Gospel of John, the story of the Samaritan woman, which begins, 'He had to pass through Samaria' (4:4). I was riveted. I could not read beyond that verse, repeating it over and over until I began to realize what was being communicated in this short verse. Jesus has to, indeed wants to, pass through my life and that of every other human being. It is his obsession, this 'passing through,' not missing a thing, taking in the entire sweep of a single life with penetrating love and a heart consumed with desire to heal. Whatever keeps us spiritually, emotionally, and psychologically imprisoned, Jesus wants to set us free. I came to understand this as the imperative of love—God's own love for us.

"Gradually, I began to see that in this story of the Samaritan woman's encounter with Jesus, he led her through a process strikingly similar to that of spiritual direction…. The rich symbolism of the story began to speak deeply to me as I entered into a mythic understanding of the dialogue that ensued between Jesus and the Samaritan woman. I recognized how much we are like her. What was taking place in her takes place in each of us, for her story is our story. The Samaritan woman kept coming to this well to draw water that never satisfied her thirst. She needed to return to the well again and again."

Symbol of the Well and the Fountain

"I began to wonder what this 'well' might signify in an individual's life. Ultimately, it seemed to me that the well is a very powerful symbol of anything in us that is an obstacle to growth in God and, therefore, to our own growth as persons with unique capabilities and untapped potential. That 'something' which we return to again and again, seeking to quench a pervading thirst, is but a symptom of an inner unhealed wound.

"Jesus came to the Samaritan woman with an offer of a mysterious water he called 'living water.' He said that this water would leap up from within a person like a fountain to provide eternal life (4:14). Who would not want this water? Yet how many of us are aware of its availability in the everyday realities of our lives?"

For more information on the centrality of the well metaphor, consult the Questions and Answers, Chapter 5, question 6.

Emergence of the *Nine Meditations*

Almita goes on to explain, "The actual writing of the *Nine Meditations* that make up this retreat flowed out over the course of two days. However, when I began writing I realized that I had not yet allowed this story, which was the basis of the retreat, to fully engage me. In response to this, I opened myself deeply and personally to the story. From this came 'The Directee's Prayer,' which is a significant part of each meditation. I was creating this retreat out of my own encounter with Jesus as he spoke to me the same words he spoke to the Samaritan woman. The directees who have either completed the retreat, or are in process with it, concur unanimously that these prayers express in a surprisingly precise, personal way what they are feeling as they pray and work through each of the meditations.

"This model for spiritual direction is not intended for someone who has not successfully negotiated his or her developmental issues prior to those that arise at mid-life. This model is proposed for those in mid-life or beyond, which generally speaking includes those thirty five years or older. This Gospel story tells us that 'the hour was about noon' (John 4:6). The retreat proposes that this information can be a metaphor for an individual who finds that he or she has arrived at the 'hour' in a human life termed 'mid-life.' The Samaritan woman had a history of five marriages by the time she encountered Jesus. It is not unreasonable to suppose that she was entering mid-life or even well into it at the time this dialogue with Jesus took place."

Conversion and Spiritual Direction

"… Jesus took the woman at the well through a process of spiritual direction—the dynamic of spiritual growth and conversion (see Chapter 7). The directee will experience the stages or movements in a holistic approach toward spiritual human maturity and wholeness. The resolution of one conflict or difficulty in a person's life is always a movement forward, to be sure, but can never constitute definitively the achievement of spiritual maturity and wholeness (holiness), for this is an ongoing process that extends to the end of any human life. However, every step taken toward the desire to grow closer to God and to respond to God's will is a movement in the direction of the spiritual ideal."

Almita includes the following two quotations by Elizabeth Boyden Howes to synthesize the thrust of her entire retreat (*Intersection and Beyond*, Vol. 1):

> *Whether one puts it archetypally, psychologically or religiously, there is in each one of us that which is meant to be one's most unique self, the God-given potential which help us to affirm. This means opening oneself to one's own depth. It means opening oneself to the shape of the moment"* (Howes, p. 104).

> *It is just possible that something might intervene in the petty, small, defensive, irrelevant life that most of us live, and yet we are thirsting to get out of. It is just possible that something could happen if we would be open. This is the magnificent moment. (Howes, p. 30)*

The psycho-spiritual process Howes describes is the same for those who make this retreat. Almita continues, "… Jesus led one woman to discover her deepest identity through an encounter with God and therefore he can lead us as well. This encounter with Jesus was the Samaritan woman's 'magnificent moment' because she was open to an encounter with Jesus.

"This retreat chooses to read the story of the Samaritan woman in a symbolic, mythic way as the externalization of the story that takes place in each of us, rather than presenting a doctrinal exposition of Jesus as the Messiah. The Gospel story is seen as one that can lead to wholeness (holiness) by following Jesus. Ultimately, Jesus is the true director not only in this retreat but also in the ministry of spiritual direction."

Almita especially emphasizes, "'He had to pass through Samaria.' Jesus 'has to,' wants to pass through each human life, through all that makes up human life, past and present. We need to be open to this 'passing through' of Jesus in our lives if we are to become free in a way we can not imagine…. We can choose to stay in denial over the fact that our own personal 'well' exists, refusing to listen to Jesus or to respond in whatever way is required in order to cooperate with this Messiah who wants to heal us and free us from within. He comes 'to sit at our well' in this retreat with an offer of patience, compassion, understanding, acceptance, and love, such as we have never known; he comes wanting to converse with us about many things.

"Jesus comes bearing the 'living water' that can recreate and transform our life. We need only to ask as the Samaritan woman did, 'Give me this living water, sir, so that I shall not grow thirsty and have to keep coming here to draw water' (4:15). But first, in order to receive the fullest benefit from this 'living water of eternal life,' we need to be willing to engage in the difficult work of removing, one by one, with the help of God, those obstacles, those inner conflicts of unresolved issues that can contaminate a human life like heavy stagnant quicksand, which keeps us bound and un-free. It is imperative to this retreat to be able to identify whatever is keeping us from ever quenching our deepest human thirst for God." Alluding to baptism, these living waters have a special significance for those preparing for baptism.

Almita concludes, "Jesus' 'living water' is offered as grace, strength, and hope. Once we change our course away from our well, leaving our bucket behind as the Samaritan woman did and discover the source of this 'living water,' we will not grow thirsty for what harms us and keeps us from becoming all we were meant to be. The Samaritan Woman Directed Retreat was created to help an individual move in the direction of the 'living water' of Jesus Christ."

Part II

Practical Considerations

3

Meditations: What Materials
Do You Need?

Cross-references

This section contains the actual meditations written by Almita Bey-Carrión. The translation for the Gospel of John in these meditations is from New American Bible, 1970; P.J. Kennedy & Sons, 1970. Over the years they have been refined. Besides the questions given for each meditation, additional questions may be appropriate for the directee. Suggestions on how to formulate these are in Chapter 5, question 7.

When a person inquires about the retreat, the Introduction is sent out with a cover letter, brochure, information on spiritual direction and survey (Chapter 11). At the end of an interview that determines the person is ready for the retreat, you would give the handout, "Preparing for and Working through the Samaritan Woman Directed Retreat Sessions." Chapters 4, 5 and 6 give pointers on all aspects of the preparation and facilitation of this retreat; Chapter 11 provides some of the supplementary handouts.

For the directee make a photocopy of these meditations on the front and back of card stock or regular paper. Ordinarily, at each session one meditation is processed before the next one is handed out. It may happen that a directee spends more than one session on a meditation or repeats part of a previous meditation. Determining the well, a source of dysfunctional behavior and spirituality, is a critical part of the retreat (see Chapter 5, question 6). Another essential of this retreat is listening to the response of Jesus and developing a relationship based on an honest dialogue with him (See Chapter 4, Noteworthy for First through Fifth Meditations).

Two rituals are integrated in the retreat. At the end of the Eighth or Ninth Meditation, the director may want to present a cup to the directee as a reminder to drink from the "living waters." Information on the choosing of an appropriate cup (Chapter 5, question 9) and the "Cup of Blessing" prayer by Joyce Rupp, O.S.M. (Chapter 11) are found in this handbook. A final ritual created by the directee may take place as part of the session with Meditation 9 session or at the following one. Information for assisting the directee with a ritual that captures the retreat experience may be found in Chapter 5, question 10.

Finally, a written evaluation helps the directee bring closure to his or her experience and provides you with insight and feedback about your direction. The writing prepares the person to make more significant evaluative comments at your concluding session. We have found it helpful to keep the written evaluations for the purpose of fostering professional growth, of fine-tuning the retreat, and of advertising the value of the retreat.

Resources and prayers for each section give further depth to the retreat. In Chapter 4, the section entitled "Enhancements to the Meditations" you will find a variety of suggestions. Many of these are included in Chapter 11. Sources for these further resources are found in Chapter 12.

Preparing for and Working through
the Samaritan Woman Directed Retreat Sessions

by Sandra Linderman

Please consider these suggestions to prepare yourself for this life-transforming experience.

❖ Cultivate a strong desire to meet Jesus in a deeper, more personal way. Put expectations aside and try to be open to being surprised by your encounter with Jesus. Your vulnerability before Jesus allows him to be the true director of your retreat.

❖ Spend time in prayer and reflection before working on each meditation. This will prepare you to start from a centered, honest and open place. Invite the Holy Spirit to accompany you as you journey to "the well."

❖ Pay attention to words, phrases, images, questions or memories that have "energy" for you as you read though the scripture passages, meditations and responses. Write these in your journal as well as your response to the printed questions and Jesus' response to you.

❖ Be willing to be honest with yourself and with Jesus in your journal writing so that this two-way conversation can allow for maximum growth and healing. Even though it may appear hard to trust and "hear" Jesus' response to the Directee's Prayer, you are encouraged to respond in some way. If at first you find it difficult to hear words, you might try to draw what you are feeling or draw an image that comes to you. Notice also any nighttime dreams that come during this retreat. Gradually, you will come to understand how Jesus speaks to you through your thoughts, imagination, and intuition.

❖ Remind yourself that this is not a class and there are no grades. You are doing this for your own spiritual growth. Don't cheat yourself by answering the questions superficially or at the last minute. It is important to allot quality time for this retreat.

❖ Spread out your journal writing over the time between meetings with your director. Trying to do it in one or two sittings will limit the meditative spirit that is so necessary for maximum benefit and growth. If this quieting and inner listening is a new discipline for you, it will take time to develop it in our fast-paced, busy and noisy world.

❖ Read through what you have written just before meeting with your director. This will help you see certain themes beginning to take shape. You might want to jot down any themes (e.g., healing, call, hope), feelings (e.g., fear, lack of trust, relief) or questions in the margin so you can talk about this in your direction session. These notes you take on your own writing and on the feedback given to you by your spiritual director will be invaluable in the months ahead when you return to continue processing all Jesus has done for you throughout this retreat.

❖ Finally, relax and trust Jesus to meet you where you are. **Jesus has chosen to meet you _at this moment._**

A note about the kind of journal notebook that is suggested for this retreat:

1. Organize a 3-ring binder and 3-ring notepaper with dividers for twelve sections (initial materials, the Nine Meditations, evaluation and ritual). This allows you to organize your original written responses to scripture and journal questions for each of the meditations, notes taken on the session with the spiritual director, additional pages of reflections, quotations, artwork, and anything else you create. This makes it easier to return later to specific meditations for further insight.
2. Make sure the binder has pockets to store handouts given during the retreat.
3. Bring colored pencils or felt pens to highlight your insights and themes.

Journal writing for this retreat:

Most people have written essays for school. They involve primarily the mind while creative writing involves the imagination. Journal writing as a way of prayer engages one's spirit, mind, heart, and imagination. It allows you to capture your night dreams, images, insights, feelings, past experiences, drawings, poetry, hopes and goals in no logical order. This kind of writing is called "stream of consciousness."

Let whatever comes be a part of your retreat journal. You can write this by hand or on the computer. What mode helps you to access deeper levels of yourself? In addition, your director will give you meditations that ask specific questions and will invite more focused writing. These offer you an opportunity to go deeper in your self-reflection. Many good resources are available on journal writing as a way of prayer. If you are not sure about how to do this, ask your director.

Drawing mandalas for this retreat:

A mandala is a drawing within a circle. It can be very structured or spontaneous; it can be your original drawing or a coloring of one that has already been drawn. You may use any medium you wish. You do not have to be an artist to draw one! The mandala takes on a luminous character when drawn with colored pencils, chalk, or pastels on black construction paper. Examples of content include images "seen" in a dream, colors or shapes that express your feelings, or an object that attracts you. Several techniques, including entering into meditative state before drawing, may be found in Judith Cornell's book, *Mandala*. Susanne F. Fincher who developed "coloring books" (*Coloring Mandalas* and *Coloring Mandalas 2*) with a variety of mandalas says this about them: "Mandalas have been used as a part of spiritual contemplation, ritual, and self discovery since ancient times…. Mandalas express completeness and invite us to experience ourselves as a whole being…." Drawing them can be a very peaceful, creative, clarifying and sacred time. They help express the inexpressible and draw together the fragments of your life into unity and balance. Through them you may access energy for healing and transformation. Ask your spiritual director to show you examples of mandalas.

The Samaritan Woman

Meditations
by Almita Bey-Carrión

INTRODUCTION

To the directee: Read John 4:4–42

You are about to enter into a process that is, perhaps more than anything else, an invitation to allow Jesus' love for you into your life more fully. It is an invitation to growth and conversion through encountering Jesus very much in the same way as the Samaritan woman encountered Jesus when she went to the well to draw water. What began as an ordinary day became for her the most significant day of her entire life. It was her "magnificent moment" in which her life was turned around both exteriorly and interiorly through a simple but revealing dialogue with Jesus. She would forever remember it as the day she was set free from the self-limitations that kept her from living a full, God-centered, human life.

This retreat consists of the *Nine Meditations* that lead you progressively through the entire Gospel account found in John 4:4–42, which is the story of the Samaritan woman. Each meditation is meant to facilitate your entering into the story as well as to help you identify with the Samaritan woman on many levels in ways that are personal to you. Answering the reflection questions, taking an honest look at yourself and your life, writing your answers in a journal, and sharing with your spiritual director all that transpires as you pray these meditations, is the best way to respond to Jesus at this time.

Each meditation is an exercise in prayer for it is in prayer that the most transforming dialogue between ourselves and God takes place. What is required is a willingness to be led by God to a new place in your relationship with God. What is required is an attitude of openness and vulnerable receptivity that renders you pliable in God's creative hands.

There needs to be a deep desire within you to move forward toward God, allowing God to move closer to you. Unlike the Samaritan woman, you know who Jesus is as you agree to this encounter. Jesus wants to reveal himself to you more fully and more personally. Jesus wants you to know him and his power in your life beyond what you may believe is possible. He wants you to experience him as the one who frees you, calls you to conversion, and reveals your mission in service to God's kingdom. Jesus offers you in this retreat what he offered the Samaritan woman: the "living water" that alone quenches the deepest human thirst, which is the thirst for God.

Enter these *Nine Meditations* with joy because Jesus has called you to this dialogue with him. Remember that Jesus "has to" meet with you, meaning he ardently desires to do so. Remember, too, that this is a symbolic approach to this story. Its rich symbolism must be entered into and must be allowed to speak to you. The dynamic of this retreat occurs in the dialogue that will ensue between you and Jesus. These *Nine Meditations* ask that you listen to your deepest self where you will become aware of Jesus' self-communication. Try to get in touch with Jesus' words to you by writing out the last section of each meditation called "Jesus' Response to You."

Because the Holy Spirit is the Mover of your soul as you work through your responses to Jesus, pray to the Holy Spirit before you begin each meditation. Ask that you be truly receptive to God's graces as God leads you toward a new place in your life.

The Meditations

These meditations are offered as a way to help you enter the story. Remember that you are being asked to identify with the Samaritan woman—that is, to recognize the ways you are like her. These meditations are meant to help you uncover the rich symbolism found in the Gospel account. Allow the symbols to inform you of deep realities. Most importantly, engage in this dialogue with Jesus as the Samaritan woman did. Her story is yours as well.

Reflection Questions

Writing in your journal as a response to the questions will help you go deeper within your self. It is important to answer these questions honestly and without restraint or restriction. Your responses to the questions are not only your contribution to this potentially transforming dialogue with Jesus, but they are your prayer to God as well. After you have journaled, sit quietly for awhile with all you have written, thought, and felt. See it as a whole and then present this to Jesus as a gesture of your deepest prayer to him.

Directee's Prayer

This prayer may help you express feelings and attitudes you may experience as you work through the meditations. Hopefully, these prayers will be useful aids in getting in touch with your human feelings, struggles, doubts and fears, as well as your hopes and aspirations. You are encouraged to write your own prayer if what you need to express is not found there.

Jesus' Response to You

Jesus will be speaking to your heart very intimately and personally throughout this entire experience. In this part of the meditation you are being asked to try to discern what Jesus is saying to you. It may come as a word or phrase that emerges from deep within you or as a longer communication. It is important that you make an effort to articulate in some way what emerges for you at this conclusion to each meditation.

The Samaritan Woman

FIRST MEDITATION

John 4:4–6

"He had to pass through Samaria, and his journey brought him to a Samaritan town named Shechem near the plot of land which Jacob had given to his son Joseph. This was the site of Jacob's well. Jesus, tired from his journey, sat down at the well. The hour was about noon."

This story begins with a short sentence that at first glance seems to simply relate a fact: "Jesus had to pass through Samaria." The fact is that Jesus did not have to do this, geographically speaking, since other routes were known and available. Rather, Jesus' passage through Samaria has to do with God's will and plan.

Jesus "has to" pass through your life as it is today, now. Jesus greatly desires to do this for reasons that will be shown to you as you work through these meditations. In your imagination, visualize Jesus' journey through human history and time, arriving at a place called "your life today." Jesus is fatigued from his journey. Perhaps he has journeyed many years to arrive at last to this momentous meeting with you. What can he want? Why does this journey of his seem to have an aura of urgency about it? He sits down right next to a "well" in your life—a deep, dark place where you go to quench a most persistent thirst. You have been coming here a long time. You have been believing that there is no other way to satisfy your need, your "thirst."

Jesus chooses this dialogue to occur during the second half of your life (v. 6, reference to noon). He is counting on your being receptive to him in a way you have not been before. Jesus is hoping that you will hear his word to you in this most personal experience and be able to respond with your will and your heart.

Reflection Questions

1. What is this place called "your life" like today, now? What are the important elements and circumstances that make it up? Who are the important people? Describe your life in great detail. See it as a panorama. What do you see? What feelings are evoked in you as you focus on your life today? What are your concerns?
2. What do you think it has been like for Jesus to journey through your life to this day? Is there anything that could possibly cause Jesus to "feel tired" pursuing you? In other words, have you resisted him or has he had to run to catch up with you?
3. What does it mean to you to be in the second half of your life? What thoughts and feelings are evoked? What are the advantages? The drawbacks?
   Imagine yourself approaching this well that is so familiar to you. What is the well? (Keep in mind that in this story it is something that is "negative," because the well temporarily quenches your thirst.) Why do you think you keep coming here? What thirst (think symbolically) does coming to this well quench?
4. In your imagination, picture Jesus "sitting at your well." What does he look like? What is he wearing? What are your feelings as you approach Jesus? What are you doing in relationship to him. (Describe this scene with as much detail as possible.)

Directee's Prayer

Dear Jesus, I have a feeling that you have been anticipating this meeting between us for a very long time. Admittedly, I feel apprehensive, unsure and curious about your intentions. I feel somewhat uneasy and even embarrassed to find you at my well. It is a familiar place that I escape to because nothing else I know of fills my need quite like this well does. You have known about this for a long time, haven't you? You know that it covers my pain, fear, and loneliness. You know how convinced I am that I cannot do without this well in my life. Is it possible to live any other way?

Why are you here now at this time in my life? Why did you "have to" come at all? I do desire this conversation with you, yet I am uncertain and afraid. I am afraid of what you may ask or expect of me. This well is such a familiar, comfortable place! I feel that I am not alone when I come to this well. That is probably the primary reason I keep coming back here. I need what this well gives me. I cannot imagine life without it. But, here you are, Jesus, just you and me. Help me to trust that whatever will be the outcome of this time together is for my growth and for my good. You must be here for a very important reason.

Jesus' Response to You

(Allow Jesus to continue to reveal himself to you. Listen intently deep within yourself to his intimate knowledge and love for you.)

The Samaritan Woman

SECOND MEDITATION

John 4:7–10

"When a Samaritan woman came to draw water, Jesus said to her, 'Give me a drink.' (His disciples had gone off to the town to buy provisions). The Samaritan woman said to him, 'You are a Jew. How can you ask me, a Samaritan and a woman, for a drink?' (Recall that the Jews have nothing to do with Samaritans).

Jesus replied: 'If only you recognized God's gift, and who it is who is asking you for a drink, you would have asked him instead, and he would have given you living water.'"

This woman was a Samaritan. According to the Jews, the chosen people of God, Samaritans were a pagan, mixed race (being half Israelite and half Assyrian), who refused to worship at the Temple in Jerusalem. Samaritans were considered "unclean," therefore Jews could not associate with them—not even to accept food or a drink from them. Jesus, however, is not concerned here with the Jewish law or with the further impropriety that as a rabbi he was not supposed to speak to a woman in public, especially a Samaritan woman. The woman's response to Jesus request for a drink (vs. 7–9) reflects this.

This story is also about each of us because we are all like the Samaritan woman. There are things about us that isolate us from our community or from our God. There are things about us and the way we live that are less than the Christian ideal and separate us from the faith of our ancestors. (Remember that an ideal is never fully achieved, rather, it is something to be striven for.) We think our weaknesses, addictions, compulsions, wounds or sins render us "unclean" before God. Instead, they keep us from a free, full response to God's love. Notice that these do not seem to keep Jesus from us, even as those things did not keep him away from the Samaritan woman. Jesus sees beyond those things in us that cause us to feel unworthy and "outside" the realm of God. The Samaritan woman could not believe that Jesus would speak to her, much less accept anything from her.

Jesus is speaking to you in this story; Jesus is asking you for a drink. You wonder why Jesus would approach you with this request because you feel deep within yourself that you are incapable of responding to the degree he seems to indicate: he is asking you to quench his thirst. How can you possibly do this?

Jesus indicates that there are important truths you do not fully grasp or understand (vs. 10). He believes it would make a difference if you did. It has to do with a gift that God holds before you and with something called "living water." Jesus is hinting that if you did recognize God's gift to you at this time you would have no need for the "water" you draw from your "well."

Reflection Questions

1. Can you identify all that might be getting in the way of your free and full response to God in your life? What isolates or alienates you from your truest self? From others?
2. Reflect on God's love for you. What thoughts and feelings come to mind? What are your most vivid recollections of how God has manifested love for you? How have you responded to these experiences of God's love?
3. What does it feel like to have Jesus ask you for a drink? What could be his reason for asking you at this time? In other words, what do you think Jesus is "thirsting for" from you?

Directee's Prayer

Dear Jesus, this request of yours is so direct: "Give me a drink." It startles me. You seem to be asking for something only I can give you. You seem to be asking for something very personal to me. I'm beginning to fear that in order for me to quench my thirst I'm going to have to give you some part of myself that I have never released. It is something very dear to me. If I relinquish my well, then I will go thirsty.

Suddenly, I'm feeling that there is so much about you I don't know, even after all these years. Do I appreciate fully the gift you are to me? I know I take you for granted sometimes and expect you to pull me through everything because you always have in the past. I'm beginning to see that I cling to childish ways and hold expectations in my relationship with you. You are telling me now that I do not "recognize God's gift." You are holding something out to me that I either refuse to see or am too blind to see. What do I know about "living water," much less believe about it? Life can be difficult. I feel alone sometimes; I feel insecure and afraid. So, I come to my well. It comforts me. It quenches my thirst… for awhile.

I know that you are trying to communicate something important to me. I want to hear but then again, I don't. Maybe I feel you are getting too close. I feel uncomfortable and anxious, as if something is going to be taken away from me—something I rely upon so heavily. Be gentle, help me to trust in your presence and your ways in my life.

Jesus' Response to You

The Samaritan Woman

THIRD MEDITATION

John 4:11–14

" 'Sir,' she challenged him, 'You do not have a bucket and this well is deep. Where do you expect to get this flowing water? Surely you do not pretend to be greater than our ancestor Jacob, who gave us this well and drank from it with his sons and his flocks?'

Jesus replied: 'Everyone who drinks this water will be thirsty again. But whoever drinks the water I give will never be thirsty; no, the water I give shall become a fountain within, leaping up to provide eternal life.' "

The Samaritan woman does not understand what Jesus means by "living water." She knows only two sources from which to draw water: a well and a place where the water is fresh and flowing such as a spring or fountain. Her understanding remains on an earthly plane. In her criticism of Jesus, whom she feels thinks of himself as being "greater than our ancestor Jacob," she unwittingly has spoken a truth, for Jesus is infinitely greater than Jacob.

Jesus tells her that in the end the water she relies on to quench her thirst can only leave her thirsty again. Jesus is telling you this too. But he knows that like the Samaritan woman you are looking for an earthly way to satisfy your "thirst." Like the Samaritan woman you can not imagine anything else that could possibly take care of your very human need other than an equally human way of fulfilling it.

Jesus is trying to take you to a higher plane of understanding and experience. He is telling you that he is the source of "living water" that will quench your thirst forever. Jesus wants to give you this water. He goes on to say something very mysterious, namely, that the water he wants to give you will somehow become "a fountain" within you. Not only that, but this "fountain" that will flow from within has something to do with eternal life.

What Jesus has said is hard to grasp. It does not seem to penetrate your understanding any more than it did the Samaritan woman's understanding. He has just offered to give you water that not only quenches thirst forever but also grants eternal life! Perhaps Jesus is feeling frustrated or even sad to realize his point has been missed.

Reflection Questions

1. In what ways do you find yourself relating to the Samaritan woman? Do you ever doubt what Jesus can do for you? If so, what keeps you from having faith at all times in what Jesus can do?

2. The woman tells Jesus that he does not even have a bucket in which to draw this water and that the well is very deep. Think of your "well," the one you have already named. Does it feel deep inside of you at times? Why do you think this is so? Jesus does not come to your well with a bucket. What might this indicate?

3. What "thirst" does your well quench?

4. Can you imagine never being "thirsty" for whatever it is your well provides for you? Why or why not?

5. When you hear Jesus saying to you that the water he wants to give you will become a fountain within you that will provide eternal life, what thoughts come to your mind? Why do you think Jesus said this fountain will be "leaping up"?

Directee's Prayer

Dear Jesus, I am feeling confused! My well is a reliable and faithful provider when I need it to be. Now you come, sit right by it, and take no account of it. It is true that the "water" I draw from my well satisfies me only for the moment or for a little while. I do always end up coming back. My thirst seems unquenchable. My well is very deep, Lord. Sometimes it feels like a bottomless pit. In fact, thinking about it can depress or discourage me. I do wish there were a better way. I wonder what it would be like not to have to come here to this well. Where would I go instead?

Tell me more about this water you want to give me. It must be very powerful.

Jesus' Response to You

The Samaritan Woman

FOURTH MEDITATION

John 4: 15–18

"The woman said to him, 'Give me this water, Sir, so that I shall not grow thirsty and have to keep coming here to draw water.'

He said to her, 'Go, call your husband, and then come back here.' 'I have no husband,' replied the woman.' 'You are right in saying you have no husband!' Jesus exclaimed. 'The fact is, you have had five, and the man you are living with now is not your husband. What you said is true.' "

The Samaritan woman remains on an earthly level. She becomes excited and happy to think Jesus is offering her water of a kind that means she will never have to come back to this "well." But she is still thinking of earthly water for she can not conceive of any other kind. Jesus is using the word, "water," in a spiritual and symbolic way. He is referring to what truly quenches the thirst arising out of her deep inner emptiness, restless seeking, and isolation.

Suddenly, the conversation takes a turn. Jesus, who had offered the mysterious water in the first place, now seems to ignore her willingness to accept his offer. He tells her to go call her husband. The Samaritan woman admits to Jesus that she has no husband. Perhaps the fact that she had been married five times before was but the outer symptom of what was unhealed and unresolved deep within this woman. Jesus not only commends her honesty but also reveals to her his intimate knowledge concerning her life. Without realizing it, she has come to a pivotal point in her conversation with Jesus because she was able to be honest with Jesus about the kind of life she was living. The Samaritan woman is now entering into an experience of conversion.

What is required in this fourth meditation is your willingness to be as honest before Jesus as the Samaritan woman was. Your life must be laid bare before the Lord. Though Jesus already knows what you may be reluctant to admit, it is this that holds the key to the beginning of your own conversion away from the falseness of your life at this time. Jesus wants you to trust him with every aspect of your life. He wants to reveal to you his intimate involvement with your past, present and future.

What is important to understand is Jesus' primary motive behind revealing to this woman from Samaria his superhuman knowledge of her life. Jesus is not as concerned about having her turn away from her former way of life as he is in revealing to her his true identity. Jesus is trying to lead the Samaritan woman to have faith in him even though coming to this faith will result, ultimately, in significant changes in her life.

What Jesus is hoping will happen within the woman is also what he hopes will begin to happen in you. Jesus desires to reveal himself more fully to you in this momentous meeting with him. He desires to lead you to deeper faith in him that will also result in significant changes in the way you are living your life at this time.

Reflection Questions

1. What do you perceive to be the central conflict of your life at this time? From what is unfolding here in this retreat, what do you think might be unhealed or unresolved? What are the external telltale manifestations?
2. Can you begin to see or understand how this central conflict contaminates your life? How? Can you begin to believe you are not free as long as it remains? Why is this true?
3. What new or deeper revelation does Jesus hold out to you about himself? What feelings or thoughts does this revelation evoke in you? Speak to Jesus as honestly as you can about this.
4. In light of all that has preceded this fourth question, what are some significant changes you would like to be able to make in the way you live your life?

Directee's Prayer

Dear Jesus, I was not aware just how deep my well really is. Nor did I realize all I've kept hidden under the rubble of my life. You are so gentle, so patient with me. I can't even feel embarrassed or ashamed because you look at me with such understanding and love. I have never experienced such unconditional acceptance as I feel coming from you toward me. I'm not sure what I feel. This is new to me. I have had faith in you; I have believed in you. But this does go deeper somehow. I feel as if I'm being led to a new place in my life. Is this what the retreat is all about?

I desire to be converted and to come to deeper faith that leads to freedom from what binds me at this time. I want to be as open to your revelation to me as the Samaritan woman was. I'm not sure if I can be. Maybe I'm afraid I won't know what to do with my new-found freedom. I have never experienced myself "there." But I have been honest with you here, Lord. I have laid a lot of hidden things at your feet. These are the things I now realize I was trying to keep from myself, but could not be kept from you. What the psalmist said is true: "You know me and you search me…." (Psalm 139).

I am beginning to appreciate just how far your love for me has moved you. Just as you went out of your way to go through Samaria, just as you extended yourself for the Samaritan woman as if she were the most important person in the world, so do I see you doing this for me, too. Am I really that special to you?

Yes, there are things about the way I live my life that I not only would love to be able to change, but also know that I must somehow change. I am so dependent on my well, Lord. This is where I feel stuck. How can I bring about the necessary changes?

Jesus' Response to You

The Samaritan Woman

FIFTH MEDITATION

John 4: 19–24

" 'Sir,' answered the woman, 'I can see you are a prophet. Our ancestors worshipped on this mountain, but your people claim that Jerusalem is the place where people ought to worship God.'

'Believe me, woman, an hour is coming when you will worship the Father neither on this mountain nor in Jerusalem. You people worship what you do not understand, while we understand what we worship; after all, salvation is from the Jews. Yet an hour is coming, and is already here, when authentic worshippers will worship the Father in Spirit and truth. Indeed, it is just such worshippers the Father seeks. God is Spirit, and those who worship God must worship in Spirit and truth.' "

The Samaritan woman is beginning to respond to Jesus' self-revelation. It is clear to her that Jesus is not an ordinary Jew, but a prophet. However, as a Samaritan, her understanding of a prophet was that he would be someone who would uphold the Samaritan tradition of worship, which was to worship not in Jerusalem but on Mt. Gerizim.

The Samaritan woman is correct in calling Jesus a prophet, but again her understanding remains on an earthly plane. Jesus is a prophet in a way that far transcends her way of thinking of a prophet.

Jesus is revealing himself as a prophet to you as well. But like the Samaritan woman's predicament, your understanding probably does not reach much further than waiting for Jesus to say what you already know or want to hear. You want Jesus to validate your understanding just as it is, rather than challenge you to come to a fuller revelation. It is hard to be called away from your comfort zone.

Jesus goes on to express that where one worships is going to lose its significance. To be a true worshipper of God, one must be born of the Spirit of truth. The function of this Spirit is to help a soul transcend the level of earth and flesh. Only this renders a person able to worship God properly.

Reflection Questions

1. When you think of Jesus as a prophet, what does that mean to you? In what ways, if any, are you experiencing Jesus as a prophet in this retreat so far?
2. To worship God "in Spirit and truth" means that you are filled with the Holy Spirit and that all your words, deeds and actions flow from this inner spring of "living water" that Jesus comes to offer. How do you evaluate yourself in this regard?
3. Jesus says that God is seeking "authentic worshippers." What do you think this means? When are you most authentic in your worship of the Holy One?

Directee's Prayer

Dear Jesus, There is so much for me to understand, so much for me to see! Take away my resistance and my blindness. I am still bound to earth and flesh in so many ways. How much of my worship of God is mere lip service? I want to live my life as a Spirit-filled person. I want to know what really matters in life and live accordingly. I'm beginning to realize that only a deep and lasting inner conversion can free me from those tendencies that keep me from fully responding to you. You came seeking me and I must let you inside of me all the way. You are telling me that the external way I live my life must flow from this inner fountain of "living water" you are offering me. You are offering me yourself for you are the "living water" I received at baptism. Why has it taken me so long to grasp all you meant when you said that you were the way, the truth, and the life?

I have gone looking for these things in earthly people, places and circumstances. I have expected *someone* or *something* in my life to bring me the joy and fulfillment I seek. This seeking has weakened me; moreover, some part of me seems lost or dead. This is what you've come to tell me. You come looking for me in order to offer me life. I'm beginning to see that this someone or something in my life can never do that. It can never fill my deepest longings and desires. It can only keep me bound in darkness. As long as I remain in darkness I will not be able to lead others as effectively as you ask me to do.

Jesus' Response to You.

The Samaritan Woman

SIXTH MEDITATION

John 4:25–26

"The woman said to him: 'I know there is a Messiah coming.' (This term means Anointed). 'When he comes, he will tell us everything.' Jesus replied, 'I who speak to you am he.'"

The Samaritan woman has truly been open to receive Jesus' full revelation. Whatever the Samaritan hoped for from the Messiah, Jesus is that fulfillment. In Jesus that time of fulfillment is present in the moment. This Gospel story tells us how one struggling soul came to believe in Jesus. The Samaritan woman came to the full realization of just who this man is who engaged her in conversation. He is the long awaited Messiah.

You are called now to recognize this same truth perhaps in a way you've never realized before. When Jesus speaks to you, it is the Messiah who speaks. When Jesus speaks to you, it is God who speaks. He has come to offer you "living water" which has within it the power to bring about a new creation in you.

The woman says that when the Messiah comes he will "tell us everything." She is thinking of a revelation in the future, failing to understand that what she hopes for in the future is present to her now in this meeting with Jesus. Not wanting her to pass by the gift he is offering and miss this momentous opportunity in her life, Jesus reveals himself as the Messiah that she and her people are waiting for. Jesus wants her to realize fully that the fulfillment of her deepest hopes can be found in him.

Perhaps you too cannot conceive that the core issue your "well" represents can be resolved, except at some future time. Perhaps you believe that it goes so deep that it can only cease to exist when you cease to exist. You may even feel that you will carry this well to your grave. But Jesus comes to say that he is the all-powerful Messiah. He has "living water" to give you *now*. What you perceive can only be resolved at some future time, whether in life or death, is possible *now*. In offering you "living water," Jesus is imparting to you healing, fulfillment, and the creation of a new you.

Reflection Questions

1. What does Messiah mean to you? If this Messiah were to come to you today, what would you ask of him? What is your deepest hope or need at this time of your retreat?

2. Jesus is this Messiah. Jesus is God with all the power of God. Jesus has come to offer you "living water," meaning that he himself wants to be the "fountain leaping up" within you that will provide eternal life. If you accepted Jesus' offer at this time, what difference might this make for you? What would you expect the power of Jesus as "living water" within you to be able to do? What about the way you live your life would change? How might you become "a new creation"?

3. Imagine, if you can, replacing your well with the love and power of Jesus as "living water" within you. If Jesus became your well, what would happen to your existing well? How would you be different? How would your life be different?

4. Does anything in the way you responded to question #3 speak to your deepest hope or desire? If so, how?

Directee's Prayer

Dear Jesus, you want to free me. You have traveled through the darkness of my deepest, most hidden need and truly understood it. More than that, you understand and have compassion for me. How you love me! You have journeyed all this distance to find me. You went out of your way because you want me to come to you instead of to this well. You come offering me an intimacy with you I never knew about. Not like this, anyway. You desire to be one with me. You desire to be my very breath and life and heartbeat. You want to live at my center leaping up as water that not only provides eternal life for me, but for others. You want me to be a fountain from which others can drink deeply. If I accept your offer today, then the water I will have to give is yourself, Jesus. If I accept your offer, then what need will I have for my old well? It's coming down to a choice I have to make, isn't it? Choices are not always easy to make, but I don't think I've ever wanted to make the right one as much as I do now.

My own well and the water I draw there contaminate my life. It is really poisoned water that kills my most authentic, true self and spirit, little by little. I don't see this happening, but you do. Now I understand why you "had to" come. My well keeps some part of me from you, even though I thought we were close. Now I see that I can never respond to the depth of intimacy you want to have with me as long as I believe my well provides the answer to my deepest needs. Intimacy and love are the deepest human needs. This is the thirst the water in my well seems to satisfy, but it is a temporary, false solution that keeps me buried and hidden from you, from myself, and from others. Now I see this. My blindness is gone. But what do I do now? What is the next step?

Jesus' Response to You

The Samaritan Woman

SEVENTH MEDITATION

John 4:27–30

"His disciples, returning at this point, were surprised that Jesus was speaking with a woman. No one put a question, however, such as 'What do you want of him?' or 'Why are you talking with her?' The woman then left her water jar and went off into the town. She said to the people: 'Come and see someone who told me everything I ever did! Could this not be the Messiah?' At that they set out from the town to meet him."

Returning from town, the apostles cannot believe what they see—that Jesus is engaged in conversation with a woman. However, they have far too much respect for Jesus to question him about this. On the other hand, the Samaritan woman leaves her jar at the well to bring the news of her incredible experience to the people of her town. She returns to her town as a missionary who wants to bring others to this Jesus she has encountered who has told her everything about her past life. She has met the Messiah and he offered her "living water" and "eternal life." Surely he would do the same for the other people in Samaria.

Perhaps you can imagine that some persons would be very surprised if they saw Jesus talking to you. Perhaps you believe yourself unworthy of such a grace as that, and yet this is exactly what is happening here on this retreat: Jesus has come to have this conversation with you.

Like the Samaritan woman you will be sent by the Holy Spirit to "go and bring" others to these "living waters of eternal life." You are to bring others to Jesus so that they too can experience him as you have. Sometimes this mission is carried out by example. People who know you may start noticing that there is something different about you. Your joy, inner peace, and enthusiasm for life will be contagious!

When she headed for town, the Samaritan woman left her water jar that she brought to the well everyday. It seems she no longer has need of it. What do you have to leave behind or give to Jesus to be free of in order to move on in your life? Perhaps you are getting closer to realizing that you no longer need to drink from your "well."

Reflection Questions

1. Review the retreat journal questions so far. What are the trends? In colored pen underline any insights you would like to remember.
2. In what ways have you grown closer to God and God to you? What has Jesus done for you in this retreat? What does he want you to do for him? How can you quench his thirst after all?
3. How are you feeling about your well and the water you draw there? Will you be returning to it as often? Why or why not?
4. What are your thoughts or understanding now regarding Jesus as a "fountain of living water leaping up from within you?" How will you access this "living water" in the future? What barriers might you encounter?
5. What questions or issues do you still want to discuss with Jesus?

Directee's Prayer

Dear Jesus, I don't know if I am ready to "go into town" yet. I feel more like sitting here reviewing all that has transpired between us throughout our conversations these many days. This I know: I have grown closer to you. Surely the encounter of the Samaritan woman with you transformed her, making her into a new woman of faith and integrity. Surely she became one of your disciples. Therefore, I believe that she did live the rest of her life as your true follower and as an authentic worshipper. Because I believe this, I also believe that she was able to make the changes that reconnected her with her community. By following the path you opened up for her, she was able to fulfill her unique destiny.

You have shown me clearly why you came to my well and what you would like me to do with it. You offer to give me all the help, power and strength I need. Can I replace my well with the "living water" you bring me? I'm beginning to believe I can. It is possible because you are my Lord and Savior who comes to free me and give me eternal life. I accept.

And with that I am going to do all I can to live as the changed person that I feel I am becoming. You have set me on a new path and called me to a new life. Like the Samaritan woman, I desire to share this good news with others. But to follow this path, I must be willing to set down my "jar"!

Jesus' Response to You

The Samaritan Woman

EIGHTH MEDITATION

John 4:31–38

"Meanwhile, the disciples were urging him, 'Rabbi, eat something.' But he told them: 'I have food to eat of which you do not know.' At this the disciples said to one another: 'Do you suppose that someone has brought him something to eat?'

Jesus explained to them: 'Doing the will of the Father who sent me and bringing his work to completion is my food. Do you not have a saying: 'Four months more and it will be harvest'? Listen to what I say: Open your eyes and see! The fields are shining for harvest! The reaper already collects wages and gathers a yield for eternal life, that sower and reaper may rejoice together. Here we have the saying verified: 'One person sows, another reaps.' I sent you to reap what you had not worked for. Others have done the labor, and you have come into their gain.' "

The disciples are concerned that Jesus has had nothing to eat. He informs them that he has "food to eat of which you do not know." The disciples misunderstand and think that someone must have brought him something to eat. Jesus goes on to explain what meeting with the Samaritan woman was really about, namely, the work of salvation and bringing persons to believe in him. This is Jesus, only-begotten Son of God, doing the work his Father sent him into the world to do. Doing this work of salvation is Jesus' "food" in a metaphorical sense. This meeting with you has been Jesus' food too. Jesus' coming to meet you at your "well" has been in obedience to God's will and plan for your life.

Jesus, the reaper, sends his disciples to help with his work in collaboration with our God who is the sower. All work together for a common harvest: the unity of all peoples in the Kingdom of God through Jesus, the Savior of the world.

You are called to this missionary work in some way with the promise that your efforts will be inspired and sustained by the Holy Spirit. Jesus said he would draw every person to himself (John 12:32), but he asks your help in doing this great work.

Reflection Questions

1. What feelings are evoked in you as you reflect on the fact that Jesus was sent to you by the Father? That this meeting was all part of God's will and plan for your life? What is your image of God at this point?
2. How do you respond to this experience? What will you do to sustain the resolutions you have made? Rather than writing a long list, select a few key changes that will help your life move forward. (Option: do a collage that illustrates or symbolizes these goals)
3. How has Jesus led you in this retreat? To what do you feel you have been led? What is your sense of mission in life? What are your thoughts and feelings as you accept this new awareness in your life?

Directee's Prayer

Dear Jesus, it will take time for all that has transpired between us to become a part of me. I feel so humbled to have experienced the depth and breadth of your love for me. Truly, it has no limit. I have learned many important things here. You have revealed yourself to me in a most intimate way. Help me never to forget what I have heard and understood. This powerful encounter has truly changed me. Now I need to live this change. That is the challenge before me and more than anything I do want to respond to the graces of this retreat as fully as I can.

You ask me to work with even greater commitment and integrity in the harvesting of this great field of God's people. You want me to help you in the work of salvation that your Father sent you to do. Continue to send your Spirit to enlighten, guide and strengthen me. May I never grow slack in my resolve to be a true missionary for you. Continue to show me what I can do. Continue to speak your word to me.

Jesus' Response to You

The Samaritan Woman

NINTH MEDITATION

John 4:39–42

"Many Samaritans from that town believed in him on the strength of the woman's word of testimony: 'He told me everything I ever did.' The result was that, when these Samaritans came to him, they begged him to stay with them for awhile. So he stayed there two days, and through his own spoken word many more came to faith. As they told the woman: 'No longer does our faith depend on your story. We have heard for ourselves, and we know that this really is the Savior of the world.'"

The testimony of the Samaritan woman brought many people to Jesus. Thus, she became truly a missionary, an apostle. For faith in Jesus to begin, a messenger, a witness to Jesus is necessary. Then, as in the case of the people of the town, their own experience of him brought them to an even deeper and more personal faith. This faith was not based on miracles and other displays of supernatural power. The Samaritans came to the purest and most radical faith, which is belief in the word of Jesus. The Samaritans, after having Jesus stay with them and after having listened to him, knew that Jesus was truly "the Savior of the world."

Like the Samaritan woman, you can be a missionary. Your sharing of your experience with Jesus will sow the seeds of faith in many. You may never know all who have been touched by your life and prayer. Yet, for faith to be truly mature, others have to encounter Jesus just as personally as you have been doing during this retreat.

Reflection Questions

1. What has been the overall impact of this meeting between you and Jesus?
2. How has this story of the Samaritan woman been your story too? How have you related to her?
3. As this retreat comes to an end, how are you like the Jews in John's Gospel who needed to see a miracle in order to believe in Jesus, and how are you like the Samaritans who came to faith solely on the word of Jesus?
4. In verse 29, the Samaritan woman went off into town to tell the people, "Come and see..." She wanted them to see someone who had told her everything she ever did. What would you want to tell others about Jesus now after this retreat experience?
5. Do you feel that you are on the road to significant changes in your life and the way you live it? What have been some of these changes?
6. We are not told what the Samaritan woman did with her life after this encounter with Jesus. Write your own ending to this Gospel story.
7. Write your own final prayer to Jesus.

Directee's Prayer

Jesus' Response to You

Optional:

You have come to realize many things through this retreat. You have changed in important ways or at least are on the threshold of change. Consider creating a ritual that would express the insights you were given as well as how you want to live out the gifts of this retreat. This ritual can be a very powerful, meaningful witness to all that you have internalized and accomplished through this experience. Your director can help you and will discuss this in more detail if you are interested. Depending upon the location, the invited guests, and the duration, this ritual may be done as part of processing the Ninth Meditation or you may choose an additional session for it.

Samaritan Woman Directed Retreat Evaluation

Almita Bey-Carrión and I sincerely hope that this retreat has moved you closer in your relationship with Jesus, as Jesus truly is. Perhaps you understand more than ever how incredibly gifted and loved you are! Even though there are no objective criteria to measure the quality of your new found relationship with Jesus, you may notice certain indications: changes in the way you live your life with others; the emergence of deeper healing, love, guidance, creativity; more enthusiasm for life; trust in responding to your intuitions and dreams; a sense of personal confidence and inner freedom; on-going dialogue with Jesus; a regular practice of prayer and meditation; or a sense of mission. As you have begun to let go of the stagnant "well" that has been so integral to your past life, you have truly discovered welling up from within you, the Spirit, a fountain of life-giving energy.

Remember that this retreat goes on as you integrate its grace and power with the rest of your life. As you have discovered, support is important in order to establish new patterns. You may find this support and accountability in a spiritual director. Know that our prayers continue to be with you.

Please keep this retreat and those who direct it in your prayers. If you have benefited from it, be sure to share information about the retreat with others.

Gratefully, Sr. Judy Rinek, S.N.J.M.

Evaluation

Please help us know what was helpful to you and what could have been improved by writing a brief evaluation. This information will be important feedback for your director and for improving a handbook that guides his or her facilitation of this experience. Some of the areas in which we would like your comments:

What was most helpful to you about this retreat?

What was least helpful?

What, if anything, would you like to see more of in this retreat?

If you have specific suggestions about the following, please make them:

Prepared meditation materials:

Prayer, questions and resource materials:

Schedule and pace:

The listening and style of your spiritual director:

How did this retreat challenge you?

What will support you best as you go forth to live out the graces of this retreat?

Anything else you would like to add:

For our final session, please, bring the following:

❖ Reflections on Ninth Meditation
❖ Your closing prayer or ritual (could be scheduled for an additional session)
❖ This written evaluation
❖ A written statement of one or two sentences that could be used for a brochure that gives a highlight of your retreat and why you would recommend it to a friend

4

Director: What Concerns the Director Giving the Retreat?

This section contains practical pointers for the director before and during the retreat. Following it are suggested materials to enhance the meditation, and most frequently asked questions with answers.

Overview of Practical Concerns

by Linda Marie Amador

Initial Contact with a Potential Directee

A potential directee may contact any director trained in the Samaritan Woman Directed Retreat to obtain more information about the retreat. He or she may have seen a flier, brochure, or advertisement, or may have heard about the retreat from a friend or spiritual director.

Sending materials ahead to the directee:

- ❖ A brochure
- ❖ Almita's introduction to the retreat (Chapter 3)
- ❖ Information on spiritual direction (Chapter 11)
- ❖ A survey and cover letter (Chapter 11)

The **"Survey of Interest for the Samaritan Woman Directed Retreat"** helps you gather more information and determine the potential of this person before scheduling an initial interview. The other materials help the one inquiring about the retreat to determine if this is the kind of experience he or she is seeking.

If it seems that the person is a good candidate for the retreat, and if a decision is made to proceed, then you schedule an initial, in-person interview and assessment. This first interview session is usually complimentary. Advise the potential directee to allow at least 1.5 hours for the first interview. Ask the person to prepare a 1–2 page essay on the spiritual highlights of his or her life and mail, fax or email this essay to you at least three days prior to your appointment so you will be prepared. After reading the essay you may have questions that you wish to ask that are in addition to those suggested in the following pages.

Initial Session and Directee Interview

Approximate time: one—two hours

The first initial retreat session consists of an interview with the potential directee to clarify the scope and purpose of the retreat and to explore his or her reasons for desiring to make the retreat, readiness for the retreat commitment, and past experience (if any) with spiritual direction or therapy. In addition, this is a time to discuss a tentative meeting schedule and fee schedule and to allow time to clarify any questions or concerns. Be aware of your comfort level with this person and his or her spirituality. Assessing the right match of spiritual director to directee is important. One possible outline for the initial interview session is as follows:

A. Welcome the Directee

Allow directee to feel comfortable in the setting you've chosen. You may offer a glass of water, ask about his or her day, light a candle or begin with a prayer. Review the spiritual highlights essay the person should have sent ahead. Go over it briefly, ensuring that you cover questions or any areas of concern. This is a good segue into the directee assessment. Explain to the directee that the purpose of this initial interview is five-fold:

- ❖ To determine if the retreat is right for the person at this time
- ❖ To clarify the level of commitment expected of a directee
- ❖ To describe the timing and length of the retreat
- ❖ To describe the individual retreat session process
- ❖ To answer any remaining questions he or she may have about the retreat

B. Assess the Directee's Readiness to Make the Retreat

1. The purpose of assessment is to determine if the timing is right for this person to make the retreat and if he or she would make a good candidate given the level of commitment required. You will want to look for the following "red flags":

    - ❖ Major psychological issues such as depression
    - ❖ Active addictive behaviors
    - ❖ Little or no belief in God and Christ
    - ❖ Inability to focus or spend time in reflection
    - ❖ No experience using the Bible for meditation
    - ❖ Reluctance to journal
    - ❖ Dishonesty about one's feelings or out of touch with feelings

Questions to ask at this time may include the directee's experience in spiritual direction and therapy and the directee's concepts of religion, spirituality, journal work, prayer, and addiction recovery.

2. Other helpful questions to ask the directee regarding readiness may include:

    ❖ What is your attraction to the Samaritan Woman Directed Retreat?
    ❖ Why do you wish to enter this retreat at this time in your life?
    ❖ What hopes, expectations, concerns and fears do you have about the retreat?
    ❖ How do you normally communicate and relate to God? (prayer, meditation, Church, other)
    ❖ Who is Jesus for you?

Also, ask other questions about spiritual preparation as appropriate. This last question about Jesus is vitally important because the primary thematic element of the Samaritan woman scripture passage and therefore, this retreat, is a meeting and conversation with Jesus. This retreat has been a powerful conversion experience for those with a negative experience of Jesus or even a doubt about his divinity. The director will need to assess the directee's openness to changing the image, or that may become a stumbling block in the retreat process.

Note to Director: If at this point you determine through your assessment process that the directee is ready for this retreat, i.e. no "red flags" are evident, then proceed with parts C through E below. Be sure to indicate to the person that you sense his or her readiness and a potentially good working relationship together. If the result of your assessment is that the person is **not** ready for this retreat, discuss these reasons with the directee and suggest other options that might be more appropriate at this time such as therapy, guided experience in meditation on scripture, or regular spiritual direction. Several of the directors have noted that some of the directees were in denial about depression at their initial interview. When a debilitating depression surfaced later in the retreat, it was reason for termination or postponement.

C. Discuss the Retreat Process, Timing and Commitment

1. Give the directee an overview of the retreat process, the components of each of the *Nine Meditations*, and the approximate time commitment required for each meditation. Give the person the handout **"Preparing for and Working through the Samaritan Woman Directed Retreat Sessions"** (Chapter 3).

2. A tentative direction meeting schedule should be determined. The Samaritan Woman Directed Retreat consists of the *Nine Meditations*. It is important for both the directee and the director to be realistic in planning. Times and frequency of meetings will have to be flexible and depend on various commitments. Sessions may be scheduled daily, weekly, biweekly, or even every three weeks. It is a good practice for both to schedule several sessions ahead.

    Note: Monthly sessions are not recommended unless near the end of the retreat; weekly and daily sessions are rare, as they involve intensive time requirements. Before you agree to daily or weekly direction sessions, ensure that the directee and you as the director both have the time to commit to this schedule!

    Clarify with the directee that the length of each direction session is usually between 1.5 to 2 hours. Each session consists of a time of prayer and contemplation as well as:

    ❖ Examining the scripture passage for that meditation
    ❖ Reviewing the directee's journal entries for the Reflection Questions
    ❖ Discussing Jesus' Response to the directee
    ❖ Discussing issues, night dreams, questions, and blessings that have come up for the directee.

3. The cost of each session should be clarified. Let the directee know what fee you charge for each session and whether or not it is negotiable. This amount may vary for each director and directee.

4. Explain to the directee that although he or she is making a commitment by beginning this retreat, that if life circumstances necessitate, the person may postpone or end the retreat without judgment. Conversely, you as the director reserve the right to terminate the retreat. This is usually rare, if the interview process has been thorough. Giving reasons for the termination would be important for closure with the directee. **Note:** Some directees terminate the retreat in an abrupt manner by leaving a phone message or missing an appointment and not re-scheduling. You may wish to discuss ahead of time your preferred method of suspending or terminating the retreat.

    If one of the reasons is that you are not a good match for this person, others who are qualified to give this retreat may be found in Chapter 11, or on the trafford.com webpage. Should the retreat be suspended for longer than two months, it may be necessary for the directee to start over.

5. Other details about spiritual direction in general should be discussed and clarified. These include assurance of confidentiality between director and directee, permission for the director to take notes during the session (if that is the director's style, see Questions and Answers, Chapter 5, question 8), and appointment cancellation policies. Also, let the directee know that he or she will be in your prayers.

D. Allow Time for Questions from the Directee

A directee may have other questions not addressed in A—C. The person may feel anxious about beginning the Samaritan Woman Directed Retreat, especially if he or she has limited experience in spiritual direction or has unresolved religious issues. In addition, the directee may be unsure of how to begin or what is expected during the sessions. It is important to allow this person time to express any doubts, concerns, anxieties or misunderstandings. Establish, too, whether or not touch is appropriate. In this age of heightened awareness of abuse, it may be your choice not to hug or touch.

Explain that it takes time for trust to develop and encourage him or her to be honest throughout the whole process of the retreat. Invite the directee to ask you about your background and style of direction. Moreover, the person may be curious about Almita Bey-Carrión and where this retreat came from (see Chapter 2, Origins).

E. Give the Retreatant the First Meditation Set

If you and the directee agree to proceed with the Samaritan Woman Directed Retreat, give out the First Meditation and any accompanying handouts at this time. Confirm the next meeting date. Give the directee your contact information, if needed. You may want to end with a prayer.

Meditations One—Nine

Approximate time each session: 1 to 1.5 hours (times may vary)

A Word to the Director about Preparing for the Direction Sessions

Advance preparation for each session is an essential part of the retreat director's responsibilities and will facilitate the flow of the session considerably. It is important to be flexible during the session, open to the movement of the Holy Spirit and the needs and desires of the directee. While it is useful to familiarize yourself with the session's scripture passage, Reflection Questions and Directee's Prayer, do not script the session in advance. If you have not given this retreat for awhile, it is also helpful to review the notes from your own experience of the retreat and to refresh your memory on what would enhance the meditations.

Remind yourself that this retreat is ultimately an encounter with Jesus. Scripture, journal questions, and conversation with director are all meant to facilitate that personal experience. It is impossible to predict the outcome of this encounter other than to say it will be life-giving and will connect a person with an inner source of vitality and direction for his or her life, if the individual is open and willing to move on. In preparation for each of the direction sessions, the following suggestions may be helpful:

❖ Set the environment of your meeting space. Ensure that a candle and matches or a lighter, a box of tissues, a glass of water, a Bible, and so on are handy.

❖ Review any notes from the previous session regarding the directee's responses and concerns.

❖ Review the meditation the directee has been reflecting on since your last meeting, noting any essential points you may wish to watch for or discuss during the upcoming session.

❖ Collect and bring with you any additional resources or handouts you feel are appropriate for the directee, based on comments from prior sessions.

❖ Review the meditation packet the directee will need for the next session, including any appropriate additional handouts. Familiarize yourself with the contents of the meditation so you may briefly overview it with the directee.

❖ Immediately before the directee arrives for the session, allow enough time to sit quietly without interruptions and distractions to pray, meditate and center yourself with the Holy Spirit. This will make a significant difference for you and the directee during the session.

Enhancements to the Meditations

by Judith A. Rinek, S.N.J.M.

General Notes to Director: Encourage directees to see what words or phrases attract them as they first ponder the scripture and/or Almita's reflections. Before answering the journal questions, they may work with these words or phrases for awhile using free association, accessing memories, or asking, "Why is this attracting me? What about this disturbs me?" This process can be very revealing (see Chapter 8 on *Lectio Divina).*

Explain that a standard question for journal work and sharing is: "What in your night dreams has caught your attention?" Many significant dreams happen for people during this retreat. Those inclined to drawing will find mandalas very revealing as well.

Instead of re-writing the "Directee's Prayer," the directee may prefer to customize it by crossing out what is not true for them and adding their own feelings, questions, desires and hopes.

Start compiling your own file of additional handouts that you think may be useful during the sessions. Sometimes an appropriate song, quiet meditation music, or silence is a good way to begin. You will find below suggestions concerning when to use certain resources. Some of these are included in Chapter 11; an asterisk (*) indicates which ones these are. Chapter 12 contains a list of books with materials from which you could create other handouts.

Organizing a three-ring notebook with nine sections—each including one of the *Nine Meditations* and appropriate handouts and prayers for it—will make these materials readily accessible. The question and answers in Chapters 5 and 6 will give further understanding of practical concerns during the retreat.

Preparation for Meditation #1: Ask the directees to imagine looking into a well and brainstorm a list of all that they might see while peering down that deep, dark well. You may find some good images for them of the well by going to google.com, click on images and search for specific ones. You may want to explore directees' associations and experiences (both biblical and human) of *water, Spirit* and *wells.* (A good resource for *well* is Br. John of Taizè, *At the Wellspring.)* A concordance of the Bible or Bible dictionary is also useful. There are many excellent prayers to the Holy Spirit that your directees may want to use before each meditation. There are several beautiful ones by Joyce Rupp, O.S.M. from her book of prayers, *Out of the Ordinary*. However, the directee may prefer to be spontaneous in calling upon the Holy Spirit.

First Meditation: Open with a prayer of hope and anticipation. If you have a picture of Jacob's well as it is enshrined in Nablus today, see what they notice. Share *Almita's reflection on it; give out Mary Oliver's poem *"The Journey" from *DreamWork*, if appropriate. Many women appreciate beginning the session with the paraphrase of *Psalm 139 by Emily Nabholz, S.C.N.

If directees have not yet written out the highpoints and challenges of their spiritual journey, it is good to have them do this for this session. Journal question #1 (about this place called "your life") may be done as a drawing or a poem. Or they may come up with an image that gives a panoramic overview of the meditation and then fill in the details.

Many times persons misinterpret the metaphorical meaning of "well" as Almita uses it in this retreat. After all, aren't wells good to have in a desert? If directees do not resonate with question #4 in the First Meditation ("Imagine yourself approaching this well that is so familiar to you. What is the well?") at first, that is OK. Their understanding of what their well might be emerges over the course of the retreat. Remind them that it is something that may appear to be good and may have even helped them cope with challenging circumstances but ultimately it does not satisfy. At this time in their life, Jesus may be asking them to transition to something more real and life-giving even though they may not yet know what that is. Invite them to be open to the possibility of change, of vulnerability, of trusting a power greater than themselves (see Chapter 5, question 6). Tom Brown's story of *Mohini the Tiger and Marianne Williamson's *reflection on fearing our greatness are powerful.

Second Meditation: For women directees, you might read the reflection to your directee *"Imagine a Woman" by Patricia Lynn Reilly from her book *A God Who Looks Like Me: Discovering a Woman-Affirming Spirituality*. I stop at the phrase, "Imagine yourself as this woman...."; they can ponder the concluding paragraphs on their own. Consider using materials on co-dependency and alcohol recovery because addictions can be potential wells. See Gerald May, *Addiction and Grace* (May, pp. 38–39) or materials on work addiction. If a person has a difficulty in letting go, Ted Loder, *"Loosen My Grip" from *Guerillas of Grace* may be a good prayer.

Materials explaining the *Jungian concept of shadow may also be useful here or in the next meditation. Flora Slosson Wuellner in her book, *Prayer, Stress and Our Inner Wounds* has an excellent reflection on pp. 50–51 concerning the transforming of the negative powers back into their original gift. For example, "our fear, when healed, becomes intuitive, empathetic compassion and sensitivity toward others." Richard Rohr, O.F.M. in his audiotape "Men and Women: the Journey of Spiritual Transformation" integrates both the theological and psychological aspects of this transformation.

Third Meditation: Consider using these materials—*"Inner Freedom" from *Prayers from Sophia* by Joyce Rupp, O.S.M., Adrian Van Kaam's reflection *"If You Only Knew" or the quotations from Pierre Teilhard de Chardin on *trusting the process and on *entrusting ourselves into the hands of Christ. Any prayer on letting go or trusting may be appropriate. Wilkie Au's insight on rootedness or stuckness can help discernment. See his book, *The Enduring Heart: Spirituality for the Long Haul* or refer to Chapter 6, question 2.

Fourth Meditation: Use the story of *"The Cracked Pot", enhanced by your collection of magazine pictures (see discussion of using the symbolic as part of this retreat below). This meditation experience is best used at end of session. Information on creating a mandala can be helpful here or later in the retreat (information is included on the handout, "Preparing For and Working Through the Samaritan Woman Directed Retreat Sessions" Chapter 3). Suzanne Fincher in her book, *Creating Mandalas for Insight, Healing and Self Expression*, interprets the twelve psychic stages manifested in mandalas.

Fifth Meditation: The following add a great deal: *Rainer Maria Rilke, *Letters to a Young Poet* ("Letter Four") *"but I believe..." or Thomas Keating, "The Fruits of the Spirit" from *Contemplative Outreach News*, Vol. 13, #1, 2000. If they are unfamiliar with the Holy Spirit, a wide variety of excellent books are available. If a person is drawn to contemplative prayer, information on centering prayer may be handed to them. For prayer I lead them into the silence with this reflection, *"Let Your God Love You." Raymond Walker's *reflection on still waters or Reinhold Neibuhr's *Serenity Prayer may also be appropriate.

Noteworthy for First through Fifth Meditations: Using the symbolic and Jesus' Response. Expressing the symbolic and unconscious in art (such as mandala, clay, collage, poetry, music and drawing) can be very helpful to you as the director. Pay particular attention to journal question #5 of the First Meditation (imagining Jesus sitting at the well, including his appearance and clothing, but especially the directees feelings as they approach him) and the reflection on the photo of Jacob's well today. I have found that certain details in these responses give clues about how they relate to Jesus and to religion in general. Many people have been manipulated (or even abused) by religion, religious people, or religious things in the past. It is important to assure them that these are not Jesus, only interpretations (and misinterpretations). They are invited to listen to Jesus speak for himself in Scripture and depth prayer.

If you use the *"Cracked Pot" story in the Fourth or Fifth Meditation, notice what sort of images that the directee chooses before hearing the story. I show the person my collection of pictures from magazines that include flowers, water, deserts, walls, ocean and beaches. Several of these can offer a glimpse of hope and of the life-giving changes that he or she is seeking. Pay attention to dream images as well as images used as the person writes or speaks. Pay attention to words used several times in one session. A directee may be saying more than he or she realizes. If you notice these things, you can bring them up at when you sense the person is open to receiving the message. That's where you and the Holy Spirit come in!

Another area of learning for many directees is how to do the final part of the meditation, Jesus' Response to You. You may have to walk the person through this for several meditations before the directee feels comfortable and confident responding to this part of the meditation. It requires "spiritual listening" which the person may not have done before. Once the directee starts "hearing" a response, be ready to respond to questions such as: "Is this only my imagination that I hear?" or "Is this wishful thinking?" Remind the person that Jesus works in all aspects of our being; the source of this insight, image, or intuition can be discerned by its "fruits."

It is important for you as the director to discern the message. If it sounds like a theological treatise, overly sentimental, or something contrary to Jesus of the Gospel, you may want to explore how the directee got to this message and where it is really coming from. Usually Jesus' response is brief, coming from the depth of the person, and resonates as true to his or her journey. Make sure that person reaches this point in each meditation before proceeding to the next one.

Sometimes the directee "hears" Jesus' response after his or her initial encounter with the scripture passage. They may not recognize it as such until later. Keep your ears tuned to the message that may be hidden in what they write.

When directees forget or don't have time to reach this part (perhaps because they are uncomfortable with it), help them notice what is going on. Are they unable to slow down enough to contemplate? Are they afraid of what might be heard? Do the directees think that Jesus really doesn't have anything to say to them? As the retreat progresses, ask the directees about any changes in the way they pray.

Noteworthy for the Second through the Fourth Meditations: Dealing with the negative. In these meditations there is a facing of the negative—for example, what is not working in a person's life, what he or she avoids, unhealed memories, the unclaimed and unlived parts of one's life. Those who are encountering these negative issues for the first time in their life may feel sadness, pain, anger, or even a desire to escape the retreat. Or, they may resist by denial, that is, they can find only positive aspects of their life or relationship with Jesus. Remind them of Jesus' love for all aspects of their being. Also, share the hopeful and very insightful reflection by Flora Slosson Wuellner on the beauty and dynamism of healed powers within (see pp. 50–51, *Prayer, Stress and Our Inner Wounds*).

Directees may always terminate the retreat and sometimes for good reasons (such as suicidal thoughts). If suicidal thoughts are shared, it is the responsibility of the director to insist that the person get professional help. If his or her condition is not serious enough to require hospitalization and you have experience working with the spiritual component of depression, you may agree to continue with the retreat. It may be important that the person make the retreat and go to therapy simultaneously.

But if this desire to escape is mere resistance to grace, your perseverance with the directee can lead to a breakthrough. Sometimes the directee may need more than one session on a meditation. It is better not to move on superficially or too quickly.

On the other hand, notice when a directee gets bogged down with introspection. It is important for the person to see his or herself in the presence of Jesus, to know that Jesus loves the person as is, no matter what! This retreat is not about "fixing" whatever is wrong within but about Jesus offering forgiveness, healing, conversion and unconditional love. This is about being freed for an authentic life and relationships. This is about being sent out to others with the "Good News." How can the directee open up to receive these gifts more fully?

Fifth and Sixth Meditations: It is important to get in touch with past images of Jesus that are not true to the Risen Christ. Ask yourself who Jesus really is to the directee. How does that change the nature of his or her relationship with Jesus and response? How does that open the person to a different kind of future together with Jesus?

Many respond to *Thomas Merton's prayer about not knowing where you're going. Materials on Jesus and women, trust, personal value, discernment, and embodied spirituality might also bring new insight. Consider using the reflection, *"Jesus to Me…" by Mother Teresa of Calcutta or the *"The Deer's Cry" attributed to St. Patrick or materials on contemplation and centering prayer.

Seventh Meditation: You may want to open the session with Joyce Rupp's prayer *"Wordless Praise to Sophia" from her book, *Prayers to Sophia*. Directees might also find materials on goal-setting and finding one's mission helpful. The CD series by BrianTracy on "The Psychology of Achievement" is excellent on goal setting. Another good resource is *The Path: Creating Your Mission Statement for Work and for Life* by Lauri Beth Jones.

Consider using guided meditations on healing, many of which are found in Flora Slosson Wuellner's books. At the end of the Seventh or Eighth Meditation, a guided meditation on a thirsty tree, *"Empowered Vulnerability" has been a very healing experience. It can be found in Flora Slosson Wuellner, *Release: Healing from Wounds of Family, Church and Community*.

If the person is a prolific writer, you may initiate the underlining process earlier in the retreat. While the person may choose to focus on the things he or she wants to remember, it may also be useful to indicated with another color or symbol, the thoughts to release—e.g., low self esteem, "stinkin thinkin," grandiose illusions, lies, and the like.

Eighth Meditation: Consider supplementing with: *Oscar Romero's reflection on mission; the *Blessing Cup" prayer from Joyce Rupp, O.S.M. (*The Cup of Our Life*) with a unique cup (see question 9 in Chapter 5), or *"Christ in my Mind" by Janet Morley.

Ninth Meditation and Evaluation: You may wish to use a prayer of gratitude. A modification of the examination of conscience highly recommended by St. Ignatius of Loyola, *the Examen, is a good tool to give your directees for the future. It can help them discern and keep in touch with the source of "living waters." Other helpful resources may be some of the books recommended in the bibliography.

Perhaps the directee needs further information on the spiritual journey? An article by Mirabai Starr in the "Sojourners" magazine (August 2005), "A Garden of Righteousness," captures the reflections of St. Teresa of Avila. If you have not yet used Richard Rohr, O.F.M. in his audiotape "Men and Women: the Journey of Spiritual Transformation," it is very practical for both men and women.

This may be the time directees celebrate their concluding rituals or the two of you may decide to schedule another session for that.

Noteworthy for Sixth through Ninth Meditations: Shift in the retreat. Usually, a shift takes place in a directee by this point. The focus inward has led to a focus on Jesus. The directee is amazed that he or she can "hear" Jesus speaking personally. The Risen Christ becomes more real to the person; sense of the presence of

Christ moves from the external to an internal reality. Many are overwhelmed by an experience of Jesus' unconditional love. At this time the directee may discover ways to deepen his or her prayer and connection with Jesus.

By the end of the retreat, this encounter sends the person outward. Leaving her jar by the well, the Samaritan woman left for the town. Near the end of the retreat, encourage the directee to be in touch with his or her intuition about a mission in life. This is a key insight in the retreat. Sometimes, a person completes his or her awareness of this mission only after the retreat is over. The bibliography contains some books that assist a person in creating detailed mission statements, if that will help the process unfold. The journal questions ask the directee to develop goals and a support system that will sustain their implementation. You may need to remind the person that one's mission is bigger than career, bigger than one's state in life; it is one's God-given purpose and destiny. For example, a directee who was a firefighter discovered he is a "teacher" in all that he does. That insight or "Aha! moment" gave him new energy, intention and enthusiasm. It helped him decide to accept one of his nephews into his home after his sister died. He is finding himself a teacher to this teenager in so many ways!

The selecting of a cup for the Blessing Cup prayer is explained in detail in Chapter 5, question 9. During the sharing for the Eighth or Ninth Meditation, I lead this ritual prayer at the end of our session.

To help a directee create a closing ritual, offer some examples and guidance. The setting, an "altar," metaphors or symbols of the journey, prayers, music, symbolic gestures can come together to express the meaning of this retreat. Although this ritual is optional, most participate. The directee's creativity is often surprising and helps bring the retreat to closure. See question #10 in Chapter 5. Sometimes the person is not ready to end the retreat just yet and may want to spread the final meditations and the ritual out for several sessions.

Both a written and oral evaluation is helpful for your encouragement and growth in this ministry. Periodic consultation with your mentor or one of the other spiritual directors can broaden your understanding of the dynamics and resources of this retreat. Finally, in-service workshops, peer supervision and other ways of deepening your skills as a spiritual director is highly recommended.

5

Questions and Answers:
The Director

1. What qualities would enhance your ability to give this retreat?

Beyond the general qualities of a good spiritual director, the following are suggested:

- ❖ A sense of call to facilitate this special kind of retreat, which is confirmed in dialogue with an experienced director of this retreat
- ❖ Experience in working with own mid-life issues and exposure to broad range of healing resources
- ❖ Understanding of the principles of Jungian psychology, *Lectio Divina*, biblical exegesis, and the Spiritual Exercises of St. Ignatius that are underpinnings of this retreat
- ❖ An ability to walk with another in pain, in doubts, in resistance, and in new and sometimes seemingly unorthodox spiritual pathways
- ❖ A repertoire of spiritual exercises from alternative resources—e.g., dream work, symbolic association, ritual, music, art and nature as sources of meditation

2. Should you guide spouses, friends or colleagues through this retreat at the same time?

To give optimal freedom to directees, it is usually best not to guide through this retreat at the same time people who are intimately connected. Since some of their issues may involve the other(s), the directees may not bring them up to the director out of fear that these issues may be accidentally divulged to the other. It's also possible that each one may unconsciously use the director as a go-between in sorting out problems with each other. It is difficult to be completely honest with the director in this situation. Also, directors may find themselves distracted, perplexed, or unduly influenced by the conflicting stories they hear.

Some directees have found it helpful, however, to share appropriate discoveries with spouses and friends not on the retreat and have received helpful feedback for future meditations. They report that these relationships have improved because of the kind of sharing that the retreat provided. Also, those in therapy are encouraged to share their journal insights with their therapist.

3. Should you guide your own friends, family members or colleagues through this retreat?

Much can be said pro and con for guiding a friend, family member or colleague through the Samaritan Woman Directed Retreat. In my situation, Almita Bey-Carrión was the only person who knew how to give this retreat and I happened to be a friend of hers. To make it work for us we had to agree for the duration of the retreat to shift into a more professional and objective mode with each other. It may happen that a friend, family member or colleague interested in this retreat may have only you nearby as one qualified to facilitate this retreat. If so, here are a few things you may have to discuss to make this retreat time together most effective: appropriate social activities while the retreat is in progress, level of honesty, potential impact on the relationship, advantages and disadvantages of "knowing" each other, openness to further depth, dealing with painful moments, issues in the relationship that may "get in the way," and ways of being accountable to each other. Agree ahead of time to suspend the retreat if after a few meditations it doesn't seem to be working out for either of you. While the retreat may have the overall effect of deepening your relationship, there also may be reluctance in revealing too much of one's darkness to you. Even if your friend, family member or colleague cannot share all of his or her journal response to you, total honesty with self and with Jesus is essential for the retreat.

To avoid conflict of interest, to be clear of the past history and emotions of your relationship, it is best to refer a friend, family member or colleague to another qualified director.

4. At a maximum, how many people are best to guide through this retreat at one time?

The answer depends upon the time and energy available in the structure of your life and how frequently the directees want to meet. Because of the frequency of meetings, the intensity of concentration on each person's story, and the darkness and pain that one has to process and bring to Christ's healing and transforming light, not many can be facilitated at one time. For me the limit has been four.

5. What is the place for challenge or confrontation on this retreat?

Because spiritual direction is an art, it depends on the dynamics between persons and the guidance of the Holy Spirit. To encourage appropriate growth and awareness takes love; to receive and respond to a challenge takes trust. Even in the early stages of the retreat, the material is very sensitive as a person names their "well" and "central conflict." At the same time, the director and directee are just building their relationship. As directors feel a deeper knowing of their directees and a trust in their relationship, they may find that creative and gentle confrontation can be more and more helpful, especially when directees are under the spell of rationalization, denial, and other forms of resistance. This confrontation may come in the form of a prayer, question, or reflection they offer rather than a direct "hit." At times, directees are on the edge of accepting a new understanding of themselves or of Jesus and the gentle nudge assists them in the naming and claiming it. In general, resistance has to be respected. When ready, directees will take the next step in their spiritual growth.

6. Why is the identification of the "well" a key to the success of this retreat? What is the source and meaning of a directee's "well"?

As the story begins, Jesus goes out of his way to meet the woman at her familiar well. Almita Bey-Carrión, creator of this retreat, saw the well as extremely significant to the whole story and to the purpose of Jesus' visitation. She wrote the following clarification in 2004: "The well itself is a symptom of something deeper, just as a real well includes both the part above the ground that is easily seen and the deep, dark part that cannot be seen. Well water comes from deep inside the darkness of the earth, while the thirst we seek to quench comes from deep within us. I[Almita] hold that the well we keep returning to, and the water we consequently drink, covers over a core wound in the life of the retreatant. There is a thirst that needs to be quenched and the way this thirst is satiated, though temporarily, is usually in the form of addictive behavior of some kind.

"Therefore, the outer manifestations or actions can be correlated to the part of the well that is above ground, the bottom of the well to the core wound, while the water itself represents the thirst caused by an unresolved issue, usually from our past.

"A well has to be dug by someone or by several people. In other words, a well doesn't just come about by itself; someone has to put it in the earth. So it is with our personal well. It didn't come about by itself; someone, some others, or some event dug a hole in us.

"Let's look at some directees' wells. We'll call the first directee Mindy. Mindy was a widow living alone. The part 'above the ground' was Mindy's addiction to reading books while eating her meals (the part above ground and easily seen is often an addictive behavior). As the retreat progressed it became clear that what these actions were covering up was acute loneliness, which was the bottom of the well or core wound. Mindy was thirsting for companionship and intimacy. What was the genesis of her acute loneliness? This required going deeper and the final realization was painful. Mindy was the firstborn of two girls and for five years had her parent's full attention. Mindy's father was especially doting and affectionate with her, often carrying her in his arms. But when the new baby came along, Mindy felt left out and forgotten. Her little sister now became the focus of her father's attention. Feeling abandoned, lonely and rejected by her father as a child was Mindy's core wound. Though she was certain her father did not intend to wound her in this way, his actions dug a deep hole that became Mindy's personal well. Mindy shared that all her life she sought companionship and intimacy of a kind that seemed to elude her. The books she read while eating were a temporary 'fix,' giving her a false sense of companionship and intimacy. But by her next mealtime she'd need to cover up her loneliness again. Reading books during meals 'helped blot everything out,' she said.

"The well is not something superficial, recent, or temporary. Though the external behavior may seem harmless enough, such as reading while eating meals, it covers up an unhealed wound whether from childhood or the more recent past.

"A second directee, whom we'll call Sue, named her well as 'compulsive over-eating.' The core wound this addictive behavior was covering up was her thirst for love, but especially the nurturing love of a mother. This directee did not have to reflect as long and hard as Mindy to realize that being raised by a cold, distant, harsh mother resulted in a very deep well being dug in her psyche.

"I [Almita] believe that regardless of what brings people to this retreat, the naming and understanding and working through of their own personal well will shed amazing light on how best to deal with present issues or difficulties. As old behaviors and old ways of dealing or coping with situations are eliminated, then Jesus' 'living waters' can gush through our lives clearing out old, clogging debris."

When directees embrace that dark, lost and vulnerable part of themselves, they come to know more profoundly God's unconditional love for them. Their eyes are opened to this part of themselves and it becomes a gift and a resource. Out of this process, they become more compassionate and less judgmental of others.

7. What might help formulate good additional questions for the directee's journal writing?

Each meditation has basic questions on the nine sections of the Samaritan woman story. However, customized questions based on the unique dialogue with your directee have exceptional value. Some of the questions may be asked and responded to after the directee reads his or her journal responses to the previous meditation. These questions may be ones of clarification or for development of insights.

Notice the hidden messages from the directee's body language, from life circumstances, from frequent use of certain words, and from night dreams. Suggest these things as topics for further journal writing. These moments of reflection can be openers for the unconscious to speak and for the Divine to be heard in a new way. For example, at the time of my retreat both my computer at home and my computer in the office were acting strangely, picking up viruses and crashing. On top of an already busy life, I did not need that frustration! My director suggested that I go beyond the literal experience to the symbolic level: to consider how that computer saga was a parable for my life at the time. Incredible truth came spilling out of that simple journal question.

Listed in the bibliography are a few books that explore the Samaritan woman story in depth. Within them you will find other possible questions and angles to consider in working with your directee. These two in particular are worth noting: Br. John of Taizè, *At the Wellspring: Jesus and the Samaritan Woman* and Vashti M. McKenzie, *Journey to the Well*.

Another powerful journal exercise is a dialogue. For example, directees might write a dialogue with Jesus over some aspect of their life, about an area of concern regarding their body, about a dream image that seems to have a message for them, or about images in their mandala drawings.

Trust your intuition and imagination in formulating a question, a brainstorming exercise, or an art or collage experience to enhance the retreat. Try for at least one additional question for each meditation. Some meditations may call for several extra questions. All the additional questions do not need to be dealt with at once. But make certain they are covered over the process of time if they are important to the retreat experience. Write them down so you can remember them later. See Chapter 6 for questions proposed by Megan McKenna concerning a scripture passage.

8. Should you take notes as the directee is talking?

Many directors record significant aspects of their conversation with the directee *after* a spiritual direction session. Because so much content comes forth in the journal reading, some may choose to write *during* their conversation with their directees. As mentioned in question 7 above, writing down additional questions is a way to remember what you have asked directees to consider. Moreover, your notes will give you concrete material to review before you see the person again. Always pay special attention to a person's remarks on "Jesus' Response to You" and to his or her evolving understanding of the well.

If you choose to use this tool of note taking, however, it is important that you explain what you are doing and why you're doing it to the directee before the retreat begins. Make sure that the person understands that these notes will be protected as confidential. I would advise shredding them at the end of the retreat unless you plan to continue spiritual direction with the person. If you are in training with another spiritual director, specifically ask permission of the directee to share a portion of your notes with the supervising spiritual director.

In addition, this taking of notes aims at capturing concepts and key words and images; it is not a word for word document. Nothing could be more distracting than slowing down the flow of the journal reading by continually asking the directee to repeat what was said. Over the course of time, you will develop a format that is useful for you but also allows for the eye contact, deep listening and reflection that are important during each session.

9. What is the value of giving a cup with the Cup of Blessing prayer? How do you select an appropriate cup?

This ritual of gifting directees with a cup for receiving and drinking from the "living waters" has the potential for closure and for modeling ritual for them. I usually offer it at the end of the Eighth or Ninth meditation, providing that it is not the same session that they do their ritual.

Use Joyce Rupp's blessing cup prayer from her book, Cup of Life (Chapter 11). Try to find a cup with a color or design or message based on what Jesus has offered them personally as life-giving during this retreat. The cup will serve as a reminder each time they drink from it.

Examples of appropriate cup designs: beautiful scenes from nature to indicate the need for time in solitude; gardening themes for time cultivating the earth; an eagle rising and verse from scripture for confidence in a new mission; a butterfly with rich color for ongoing transformation; Scriptural quotations such as "Love is…." to remember the essence of life; a grapevine and grapes and the scripture verse, "I am the vine….," to remember to keep connected with the source of life; or even an elegant tea cup and saucer for times to pause in conversation with good friends.

10. What is the purpose of the closing ritual? How do you guide someone in deciding to do it and then creating it?

About mid-point in the retreat is a good time to raise the possibility of a concluding ritual for the retreat. If directees need more instruction or time to think about the possibilities, then they have the time to do that. For those who choose to do it, it helps to bring closure to the retreat and to celebrate the main grace of this experience in a holistic way. Creativity has abounded and this may turn out to be one of the most delightful parts of the retreat. Guests may be invited. I have traveled to other sacred places for my directee such as streams, chapels, or homes. One ritual took a directee to a holy shrine in another country. Symbols have varied such as a pigeon released, a long winding bandage being burned, a pot with many labels being left at a well. Ritual is not for everyone, however; some have ended with a simple prayer of gratitude.

In giving a directee guidance, remind the person that simplicity is important. Ask, "Is there anything—an object, song, or prayer—that symbolizes what Jesus has said to you during this retreat?" Give examples of other ceremonies. Along the way ask how his or her ideas are coming. If in the journal sharing a key image emerges, you may suggest how that would fit into an appropriate ritual.

11. Is it best to terminate your relationship at the end of the retreat?

For persons who are moving away, for those who already have a spiritual director, and for directors who already have a full number of directees, the relationship at the end of the retreat most likely will be terminated. In some cases, a person may write to you for awhile and you can assess whether to respond. Some have chosen to call or have lunch to give a periodic update on their life. At times the directee may find it helpful to continue in formal direction as some of the insights from the retreat unfold. Moving into a monthly visit with less structure takes an adjustment; you as the director can be helpful in guiding the process.

12. How can you contact the author of this handbook or other spiritual directors for clarification, further information or consultation?

In Chapter 11, is the phone number for the author, Sr. Judith A. Rinek, S.N.J.M. Periodically, this information will be updated on the handbook web page (www. trafford.com) and in future editions of the handbook.

13. What "obligations" or conditions are attached to using these materials?

Before giving this retreat, you are encouraged to make this retreat with a director experienced in giving it. This person may become your mentor as you discern your call to facilitate this process in others (see question 17).

Chapter 4 will help you prepare yourself well for each session of the retreat. At the end of the retreat, plan to go over with your mentor the evaluation written by the directee. When you become confident and experienced in successfully guiding others, you may want to add your name to a common brochure advertising the retreat and to the web page for this handbook.

To obtain the meditations and permission to copy them, to find helpful resources, each director of the retreat will purchase this handbook. With it comes an option to consult with its author Sr. Judy Rinek, S.N.J.M., and other spiritual directors facilitating the retreat.

Since this retreat by Almita Bey-Carrión is copyrighted, materials are to be used according to her specifications—that is, that this retreat be facilitated by a spiritual director in a one-to-one context and that her sequence of meditations and journal questions (with your enhancements) be followed. You, as the bearer of this handbook, are the only one who has permission to duplicate retreat materials for your directees. Because of the copyright on these materials, it is not lawful to duplicate copies of this handbook to those who have not purchased it.

14. **Why is this retreat designed for one-to-one facilitation? Couldn't it be adapted for a group?**

Anyone with a gift for facilitating group spiritual direction and meditation could organize a day or several days of a group retreat. The advantage of taking the story of the Samaritan woman in a group is that more people would have an opportunity to meditate on this scripture and benefit from the faith reflections of others. One disadvantage of the group process is that the trust needed for deep honesty and insight takes a long time to build. Another is that the group process may not meet all the participants where they most need inspiration, feedback, challenge or encouragement. If persons do not feel comfortable sharing their "well" with a group, they would miss the most critical part of the retreat. Finally, some seem to discover pain or resistance within themselves at different points and may need to stay with that particular meditation longer. In a group setting this is not usually possible.

Those who prefer a group retreat format can find two excellent ones in the book written by Miriam Malone, S.N.J.M., *Enter the Rose: Retreats for Unfolding the Mysteries of Faith with Catechumens, Candidates, and All Believers*. Originally designed for catechumens and their sponsors during the faith formation process called Rite of Christian Initiation of Adults (R.C.I.A.), it can be adapted to any prayer or faith-sharing group. One retreat explores the theme of individual and communal thirsts and the other explores conversion stories and calls forth liberating action. The questions identified by Megan McKenna in her book *Not Counting Women and Children: Neglected Stories from the Bible* (see Chapter 6, question 16) also lend themselves to a group experience.

Almita Bey-Carrión has specifically designed this retreat to be a very personal dialogue with Jesus that leads to conversion. Christ speaks to directees in their personal journal work, in their contemplative listening to scripture and to the Spirit within, and in their dialogue with their spiritual director. The Holy Spirit infuses the whole process with surprise, energy, and enlightenment. Even though each meditation has common journal questions, for each directee the spiritual director customizes additional journal questions, prayers, and resources. Moreover, many take longer than the ten sessions to complete their unique walk with Jesus and the Samaritan woman. At the conclusion directees are invited to facilitate a closing prayer and ritual that best expresses their journey.

Directors who first make this retreat before directing it will be equipped with a personal experience of the dynamics of conversion that unfolds throughout its individualized process. From this experience they can understand more clearly why its dynamic and impact cannot be duplicated in a group setting.

15. **What materials are essential for the retreat and what is up to your resourcefulness and creativity?**

Materials that Almita Bey-Carrión has developed, namely the introduction to the retreat and the *Nine Meditations*, are all that are really necessary for this retreat.

Over time, certain prayers or reflections have accumulated because of the resources of each of the directors. The following are some examples. At the end of the Fourth Meditation, the story of the cracked pot and the selection of a photo seems to give hope about how God works around weakness and sin. Near the end of the retreat, the "Blessing Cup" prayer of Joyce Rupp, OSM, along with the gift of a special cup seem to be an effective way to bring closure and give a constant reminder to keep drinking from the "living waters." Many of these resources are published in Chapter 11. In Chapter 4, "Enhancements to the Meditations," many recommendations are made for each meditation. In addition you are encouraged to gather material from your own experiences of the retreat, from personal resources, and from resources in the bibliography.

One way to keep the appropriate resources for each of the meditations at one's fingertips is to organize them in a three ring binder. Make a section for each of the meditations. In each of the nine sections, insert in plastic pages (one handout per page) the materials that you may want to give your directee for further reflection or prayer. Keeping a file with extra copies of these resources is both handy and efficient.

16. **How do you get the word out about the nature of this retreat and your availability to give it?**

Five ways have been effective in spreading the good news about this retreat:

1. Personal recommendation to friends by those who have completed the retreat
2. A mini-retreat and information session—including an experience of *Lectio Divina* meditation, information on spiritual direction, and the testimonies of a few people who have already made this retreat
3. Suggestions to others who might benefit from this experience, especially those in discernment or in recovery from addiction, co-dependency, or in mid-life transition
4. Announcements or fliers in retreat houses or church mailings
5. Listing your contact information in the general brochure on this retreat or on the handbook web page

17. **What process is used in training another person to give this retreat?**

Almita strongly recommends that potential spiritual directors make this retreat before they are qualified to facilitate it for another (see Chapter 7, Critical Guideline). The second recommendation was that interested persons already be trained and experienced in the art of spiritual direction. After the retreat and after a sufficient time for integrating its graces, you as a potential director would seek out an experienced director for discernment. Discernment would include the following:

❖ A sense of being called
❖ Clear indication from the Spirit that you are asked to do this for others
❖ Evidence of having integrated most of what you discovered during your retreat
❖ Ability to support the transformation process of your directees during the retreat

Potential directors would arrange to be supervised by this experienced director while giving their first Samaritan Woman Directed Retreat. Afterwards, any further desire for supervision or mentoring would be assessed.

For a group of on-going directors, peer supervision has also been effective. Supervision groups can be organized by those living in proximity to one another. A helpful resource for developing a format of supervision is Maureen Conroy, *Looking into the Well: Supervision of Spiritual Directors.* Our group has included some discussion around the retreat in addition to the supervision of our experience in spiritual direction.

Remote preparation for giving the retreat (see Chapter 4):

1. **Read:** this handbook and background resources
2. **Review:** your own experience of the retreat and the copyright agreements
3. **Gather:** materials and resources for prayer

The directee should be informed if you are giving this retreat for the first time. Also, you would secure permission to share their responses with your supervisor. Your supervisory conversations would be confidential.

In addition, your supervisor and you would agree ahead of time on the kind of communication that would help you prepare for and learn from each session. This handbook provides all the necessary meditations and background material for you. At the end of the retreat the conversation between you and your supervisor would review your evaluation of the directing experience as well as the evaluation of the retreat from the perspective of your directee. From there next steps would be developed.

6

Questions and Answers: The Directee

1. **Does a person interested in this retreat need previous experience in spiritual direction?**

Previous experience in spiritual direction is helpful but not necessary. The advantage is that persons in direction understand the nature of it and how to prepare for it. Moreover, after this retreat their regular spiritual director can assist them in their ongoing discernment and integration.

What is most important, however, is a person's readiness for the Samaritan Women Directed Retreat, his or her ability to be reflective, and a commitment to make time for all aspects of the retreat. If needed, a few spiritual direction sessions before the retreat would prepare a directee for the daily discipline of scriptural prayer and reflective writing, and would further clarify what is already being dealt with and what needs to be set aside. This may also help develop trust and comfort with the process of disclosing personal information to another.

2. **If potential directees are already in a spiritual direction relationship, what are the indications that this kind of retreat would facilitate their spiritual journey more than traditional spiritual direction?**

This retreat opens up a person's life in more depth than traditional, monthly spiritual direction. It provides conditions for a growth spurt. When a person desires to go deeper in prayer, feels stuck in his or her relationship with God, feels confused about a future direction, wonders about making a major move in career, relationship, lifestyle, is wrestling with various mid-life issues, or is recovering from the effects of addictions or illness, this more intense and structured experience can give support and guidance to growth. Essentially, when one finds that much of what worked in life before no longer works, now is the time to move into this retreat.

Wilkie Au in his book, *The Enduring Heart: Spirituality for the Long Haul*, has a very clear description of what "stuck" means:

❖ *stuck when we let past failures, poor decisions, missed opportunities make us unforgiving of ourselves and cynical about life.*

❖ *stuck when we hang on to resentments toward those who have wronged us and let these resentments chain us to frustrating relationships.*

❖ *stuck when we let ill-health and the normal aches and pains of growing old make us crabby and less appreciative of the small blessings of daily life.*

❖ *stuck when we do not seek help for healing the poor images of the self resulting from childhood traumas that hamper our present lives.*

❖ *stuck when we let envy of others consume us rather than gratefully acknowledging our own blessings and developing our own gifts.*

❖ *stuck when pain and hurts from past intimate relationships keep us from being loving and vulnerable.*

❖ *stuck when fear of failure prevents us from trying new things.*

❖ *stuck when anger about past disappointments and losses cuts us off from reconciliation with a God who wants to be close to us.*

❖ *stuck when we let fear rule our lives. (Au, pp. 11–12)*

The Samaritan Woman Directed Retreat enters the inner life respectfully, safely, and methodically. It provides a solid spiritual foundation, connects with a divine energy and builds a relationship that may have been inaccessible to the person before. Provided that no impediments are present in the directee, this retreat may be an excellent next step.

3. What are the indicators of readiness for this kind of retreat?

A director should look for the following in the directee in the initial interview:

❖ Consciousness and confrontation with mid-life issues
❖ Desire and motivation to get beyond the "dead" or stuck areas in one's spiritual life
❖ Need for discernment in life decisions—e.g., religious life, career change, baptismal preparation, recovery from addiction or illness
❖ Openness to writing in a journal and a willingness to share it
❖ Ability to set aside quality time for reflection and response to the retreat materials
❖ No major psychological or spiritual barriers (see question 4)
❖ Courage, integrity and honesty with all aspects of oneself
❖ Sensitivity for one's inner life—imagination, feelings, intuition, desires, images, thoughts, fantasies, dreams, motivations—and an ability to articulate what one finds
❖ Desire for a real relationship with Jesus and an openness to go beyond past conditioning and stereotypes
❖ Experience in *Lectio Divina*

4. What are "red flags" concerning the unsuitability of the person for this retreat?

Those who should be encouraged not to make the retreat are those who:

❖ Have recently been traumatized by divorce, abuse, terminal illness, violence
❖ Are living with an active addiction, especially with drugs or alcohol
❖ Are clinically depressed, or have a serious mental illness
❖ Reject Christianity or the possibility of a relationship with the Risen Christ
❖ Have not begun a spiritual life or developed a regular pattern of prayer
❖ Fear God unduly or have strong misconceptions about God

> ❖ Are unable to be candid or articulate about one's inner life
> ❖ Have a personal agenda that is radically different from the purpose of the retreat
> ❖ Are too busy or whose life is complicated by unexpected demands on time and energy
> ❖ Are unable to trust another person

Refer to the information on "Initial Session, Directee Interview" in Chapter 4 as well.

5. **Should a person in therapy make this retreat in addition to therapy?**

This retreat has been completed successfully by those who were in therapy because none of the "red flags" were present.

Initially, a person considering this retreat should discuss the possibility of concurrent therapy and the Samaritan Woman Directed Retreat with his or her therapist. For one who has the time and energy for both processes, the retreat greatly enhances the healing because it consistently addresses the spiritual core of the person. The director encourages the directee to share journal responses with the therapist, when appropriate, and the director may recommend that certain issues which arise during the retreat be addressed further in the therapy process. Incidentally, some who finished psychiatric treatment for depression or abuse found that this retreat deepened their healing.

6. **Is it advisable that the directee suspend sessions with his or her regular spiritual director during this retreat?**

Many times the person beginning retreat is already in spiritual direction with you. Thus, the monthly sessions would be suspended during the retreat and resumed after the retreat. Some of your future work together would be to notice how the grace of the retreat continues to unfold.

If the person has another spiritual director, he or she would have a conversation with that director to discern what would be appropriate. Some do not have the time to do both; others have found the feedback on his or her retreat experience from a long time trusted director to be most valuable. Whether direction is suspended for the duration of the retreat or not, the eventual sharing of the material of this retreat with a person's regular director is strongly encouraged. It will strengthen and integrate the experience.

7. **If persons have not had much experience in prayer, what would be a helpful preparation for the retreat?**

Several issues need to be addressed for persons who do not have a regular prayer life. First, discern if this inexperience in prayer is due to lack of religious education or to something closer to a "red flag", such as resistance to a relationship with God, busyness, misconceptions about God or prayer, or an inability to discipline themselves. Persons who have not had an opportunity to learn how to pray may need a period of preparation before the retreat. Besides recommending helpful books or workshops on prayer, the director may wish to have several sessions to mentor such persons in using the *Lectio Divina* style of meditation.

8. **When a directee brings a specific agenda to the retreat, when and how do you deal with it?**

Some persons' agendas have been so strong that they were not able to fully concentrate on the main focus of the relationship with Jesus. They ended up dropping out. That agenda can be an unrealistic view of the retreat or one of the "red flags" above. Once the purpose of the retreat is understood, the director and potential directee can ordinarily see if there is any possible connection or enhancement that the retreat can offer.

In my experience, those who suspended their agenda at the beginning of the retreat had greater clarity when the retreat was over. Often the Spirit surprised them with new resources to move ahead. For example, one directee connected with potential partners for creating a retreat center during the course of the retreat and was handed a house free of charge soon after the retreat was over. After five years, this retreat center is still flourishing. She began the Samaritan Woman Directed Retreat concerned about how she was ever going to finance such a project! Unfortunately, another directee could not suspend her agenda about deciding on her next career move. When a job opportunity arose early in the retreat, she could not resist the temptation to take it. With the new position she no longer had the time or the reason to continue this retreat. Later on when the position turned out to be the wrong one for her, she contacted me saying that she regretted not finishing the process of the retreat in order to discern where she was truly called.

9. How much time should pass between sessions with you and the directee? What are the maximum and minimum time periods?

The amount of time between sessions will depend on the individual, the circumstances in each person's schedule, and the particular section of the retreat.

For a person who is ready and wants to enter deeply into the meditations, the retreat can be given daily for ten consecutive days, with each day being devoted to one set of journal questions. Often I recommend that very busy people take ten days off to make this retreat, since finding time amid their regular schedule is often difficult. After such intensity, however, I suggest that these persons review the whole retreat with their regular spiritual director for several monthly sessions. This helps to integrate their insights on the retreat with the realities of daily living.

Ordinarily, directees meet every other week with their director. This gives them time to meditate and write their journal reflections in the midst of their daily activities. During times of crisis or because of deadlines (vacation ending, personal or professional needs, and so on), a weekly or daily meeting can be arranged, providing that they can spend quality time on the meditations. At the beginning of the retreat, it is best to meet with shorter spaces of time in between. Near the end of retreat, especially if the Seventh through Ninth Meditations take place during the summer, the meetings may be three weeks to a month apart.

When the pauses are longer, it is difficult to keep focused on the retreat. A person who has begun the retreat and then paused more than three months may have to start over.

10. Some questions may seem repetitious to directees. Should you eliminate these questions or have them ignore the ones that they think they have already answered?

Spiritual guides such as St. Ignatius of Loyola talk about the importance of repetition:

> *For Ignatius, a repetition is never the simple reduplication of a prior exercise, not a simple review of matter; rather it is a return to and a dwelling on those points where affective responses of spiritual experiences were stimulated: consolation, desolations, inspirations, etc. What is repeated is not subject matter, but points of notable sensitivity (or lack thereof), so as to reinforce, deepen, or better appreciate....*
>
> *By repeatedly entering the mysteries of the Lord at successively more intimate levels, a person can be expected to see, savor, and know the Word in a new and wholly personal way....*
>
> *The process might be compared to focusing closely with a zoom-lens, which eliminates large areas of the original picture so as to concentrate on points of particular interest... 'It is not much knowledge that fills and satisfies the spirit, but to feel, and taste things inwardly.'*
>
> *Ignatius does not aim his repetition at expanding concepts, spiritual theology or noetic faith, but rather at simplifying and intensifying an awareness of spiritual realities, especially personal presence to and service of the Lord (Asselin, pp. 293–294).*

In this retreat, the spiritual realities of drink, thirst, spirit, and "living waters" are asked about repeatedly which intensifies the awareness and meaning of them. They also provide for an even deeper conversation with Jesus regarding these spiritual realities.

There is another reason for repetition as well. Although certain concepts about the negative in our life are probed again and again—e.g., the well, the central conflict, barriers—each time they are brought up, directees get a deeper and more nuanced way of understanding what gets in the way of their full life and destiny. Even more importantly, they feel keenly the absence of Jesus' presence or their resistance to him and his ways. As directees are asked to identify in different ways what the "living waters" feel like, they are invited each time to focus more clearly and realistically. They note the changes they experience and then finally discern what goals will help them move forward. Each time they will notice where the life is bubbling up in them and what their energy, enthusiasm, hope, and love center around and things will become clearer. These answers may take several explorations if their "treasure" is buried deep in the subconscious.

11. How do you deal with parts of the meditation that the directee seems to have left out, skipped over, or treated superficially?

Directees need to know that all aspects of the retreat are important for its dynamic to take hold. At times, I may ask them to finish a meditation, or to write down something they started to answer spontaneously in our session together. If incomplete meditations occur consistently, I may encourage them to take enough quality time for this retreat so they can get the most out of it. Sessions may have to be scheduled with longer intervals in-between so they can enter the meditation more completely.

I might also ask myself these questions: Is this pattern part of the person's resistance to Jesus? To spiritual growth? Is the retreat getting too close to issues the person is not ready to deal with? If this is true, it is wise to raise the possibility with the person, but not force him or her beyond the discussion of it. Inviting the directee to respond to the question with artwork or other symbolic communications may fit better with his or her learning style or even help the person get beyond ego defenses to a deeper truth. At times a guided meditation or meditation using music can open the door to the directee's inner life. Continue to look for signs of readiness to move on.

Signs of readiness for growth include: the person growing tired of the same old patterns or seeing clearly how those patterns do not work anymore, bringing up intriguing dreams, noticing that new visions, desires or energies are spontaneously bubbling up within.

12. How do you respond to the unique spirituality of men who make this retreat?

The approach of this retreat may seem foreign to men who are not in touch with their inner feminine because the "hero" of this biblical story is a woman or because the creator of the retreat is writing out of her feminine experience of spirituality or because much of the retreat involves reflection on their inner life. One man who made this retreat successfully could access the deep feminine side of himself through his relationship with Our Lady of Guadalupe. Since the development of the feminine side of their personality from the Jungian perspective is an important development for men in mid-life, there are ways of reaching out to those who would be open and ready for this experience. Men who have been in therapy or Twelve-Step programs have usually developed the necessary honest self-reflection and effective communication skills.

Moreover, many men have a difficult time accessing their emotions or articulating them. Their challenge is to move from the head to the heart. If they have accumulated hurt, pain and anger for many years, or have moved into denial, bitterness or depression, they may need therapeutic intervention as a way of preparing for this retreat.

Also, prayers that refer more to a woman's experience have to be modified or substituted. When the director confronts a man in direction, he responds best to a direct and clear approach with many concrete examples. He is less inclined to comprehend the symbolic, metaphorical and poetic aspects of the story and is more responsive to elements from scripture study. For example, he may approach the issue of "many husbands" (v. 18) in a different way than a woman would. The director could be effective with him by presenting the opinion of scripture scholars that the passage referred to the many pagan gods that the Samaritans worshipped because of their history of intermarriage. So these questions can be raised:

❖ What are your "idols"—that is, what takes most of your energy and time? What are the overall
    effects of your choices?
❖ Are there any inappropriate relationships with women outside of your married relationship?
    Celibate lifestyle?
❖ How much of your self-image is wrapped up in what you do rather than who you are?

Instead of the woman at the well becoming a personal hero for men, she becomes an example of faith, conversion and discipleship. Through her the male directee will come to appreciate Jesus' regard for women. In addition, her unique situation of being regarded unworthy, alienated and invisible is still true for the "feminine" qualities within males. That truth comes to a new level of understanding for those unaware of how a male-dominant society and church have impacted both men and women. Jesus has a message for males concerning how they honor and integrate the feminine within and how they deal more compassionately with the women in their life.

I have met men who fear that if they go into a retreat such as this, their spouse will be "left behind" in spiritual growth. (It is interesting that most women do not express this concern when they choose to make this retreat.) First, this concern has to be explored as a stalling tactic or resistance mechanism to making the retreat. You can encourage him to share his insights with his wife and to write in his journal her responses to his insights as well. See Chapter 5, question #2 about the wisdom of both husband and wife making the retreat at the same time with the same director.

13. What are the signs to terminate a directee's retreat and how can it be done gracefully?

At the beginning of the retreat, directees are told that they may end the retreat at any time. Since they pay as they go, they will not have lost out financially. This gives them freedom to stay or leave for whatever reason. Most people find this retreat more revealing than they expected and there is usually a point in the retreat where a difficult truth emerges. At that point, some resistance, fear, and sadness may set in, but usually that does not last for a long period of time. However, some directees may choose to go no further.

The most common reason for not continuing this retreat is that persons discover that they are much too busy to put quality time into the meditations. They usually terminate the retreat without much prompting. If a person keeps rescheduling appointments or not showing up, that is a time to initiate a conversation about what is happening. It may be a sign of temporary resistance, or an unusually busy time, or it may be an indicator that this retreat is not for him or her. A few have had a difficult time admitting that. Usually, the person is glad when a mutual decision is reached for termination.

If a "red flag" such as depression did not surface in the initial interview, it may come up at a difficult moment in the retreat. For example, one directee started to have suicidal thoughts. At this point the director referred this directee back to therapy for more in-depth work and postponed the retreat until the person was ready to return to the retreat.

It may become clear to a directee or the director that the "fit" is not right for the two people to work together. Hopefully, the incompatibility is assessed in the initial interview and a referral can be made to another director of this retreat. If it comes to light later and the directee wants to continue with a new director, then let the person know who else is available. It is up to the directee to make the contact and, usually, he or she would start the retreat over with the new director.

14. What have been the outcomes of this retreat?

The most consistent outcome of this retreat has been a deeper relationship with Jesus, especially a regular habit of communication. Many were led to contemplative prayer as a deeper way of listening and to taking quiet time as a balance for a busy lifestyle. Women especially have come to trust God more and act upon the inner nudgings of the Holy Spirit. Those who had doubts about the reality of Jesus have come to experience his divinity in a profound way.

Since this retreat was designed for those in mid-life transition or those stuck in their spiritual journey, healing has been another frequent outcome, especially for those dealing with the residue of depression, abuse, or addiction. Several have expressed a feeling of "coming home" to themselves—that is, living their own lives with greater integrity and zest. Many have become clearer about their mission in life and have gone forth with anticipation and confidence. From their retreat experience, they came to believe they could count on the presence, energy and love of Jesus no matter what the future brought. They were enabled to leave behind past habitual thoughts, feelings and actions that no longer fit what they had come to know about themselves and about Jesus.

Through this retreat these graces are a sampling of what has happened over the years of this retreat—finding the courage to leave an adulterous relationship, accepting the limitation of illness and aging and finding the blessing of compassion there, final release from depression, discovering creativity within, beginning one's education toward a new ministry, healing the scars of sexual abuse, coming to value oneself and one's life experience, establishing a retreat center for women, connecting to a source of power and guidance within, and sensitivity to Jesus' love and presence.

More and more persons in recovery from cancer and other life-threatening illnesses have been attracted to this retreat. Since their illness forced them to re-arrange their values and priorities, they have discovered through this retreat how to live this second chance at life. Life for them has become a precious gift.

15. What enhances the unfolding of the grace and insights after this retreat has been completed?

The answer to this question is as unique as the experience that has taken place during the retreat. What does the person feel would continue the transformation begun during the retreat? Some directees who already had a spiritual director found it helpful to continue the process of integrating their insights with that director. A few continued with the director of this retreat for ongoing spiritual direction.

Within the retreat are questions about the steps directees will take, the barriers to taking those steps, and how they plan to overcome these barriers. The director and directee must insure that those steps chosen are realistic and motivating. Directors might ask these questions of directees: Did issues arise that require psychotherapy? Do they need to study further on a certain topic? Are they willing to continue keeping a journal to reflect further on revelations, issues and resolutions made in the retreat? What are their "triggers" or times of vulnerability to the old behaviors? How can these be dealt with effectively?

Since the retreat encourages directees to listen consistently to Jesus speaking to them, they will find that continuing this dialogue through journal writing, meditation on the Gospel, or contemplation on a daily basis will keep them in touch. A modified version of the examen of consciousness may also be adopted. The directee may also connect with a support group, Twelve Step group, journal group, prayer workshop or others who have made the retreat.

Directees may also review their journal from the Samaritan Woman Directed Retreat on subsequent personal retreats. This review can become a touchstone for further growth. In general, it helps directees to re-read their journal four to six months later, a year later, and two years later to see where they are and what needs to be integrated further into their life. Each time they return to their retreat journal, they can add pages or notes about new insights, opportunities, and challenges. Goals established during the retreat may be modified or new strategies would be developed.

Almita added the following in 2004: "It is important for directees to realize that whatever door to healing was opened, it is a process that may continue for a long time. Furthermore, whatever tempts directees to go to their "well" is something they will always have to guard against. Self-scrutiny is important, which is how ongoing spiritual direction, prayer, and journal writing can help the graces of the retreat to be integrated fully.... Approaching life one day at a time has proven to be a successful way to keep addictions and weaknesses from regaining control. The retreat is best carried forward by directees' resolve to keep away from their well one day at a time. This effort along with energies directed toward new goals can help directees remain open to the 'living waters' Jesus came to give."

16. Why have some chosen to make this retreat more than once? What would be helpful in facilitating this retreat the second time around?

While many have seen this retreat as a once in a lifetime experience, some have returned for various reasons. To name a few:

❖ To finish the retreat
❖ To gain clarity with a new transition, obstacle or issue
❖ To heed an inner attraction or call for a more intimate relationship with Jesus
❖ To process and deepen the growth begun in the first retreat
❖ To return to the dynamics of the retreat in preparation for becoming a spiritual director
❖ To pick up what they might have missed
❖ To deal with a new "well" or a different level of their present one
❖ To identify further the mission or destiny that is emerging

Their motivation may be discerned with whatever is appropriate in the following questions:

1. Be specific about what you are <u>looking for</u> and <u>looking forward to</u> as you return to this retreat—expectations, concerns, feelings.
2. What has stayed with you and developed since your first retreat? How did you process the retreat afterwards? Do you still have your journal and handouts?
3. How have your earlier insights influenced your daily life? If not, what would make the difference this time?
4. What issues in your life are asking for more examination or feel unresolved?
5. If you did not complete the retreat, what was happening in your life that led you to make that decision? What would support completing your experience this time? Are there any indications that you are ready to do this? Do you feel it is best to begin again or to get back into the "flow" of where you left off and continue?
6. How did you pray before the retreat? How do you relate to Jesus now? What mode of prayer has emerged within you since the retreat?
7. What best facilitated your growth during the past retreat experience? What got in the way of your growth or made the retreat difficult? Is there anything you would like to see changed as you return? Do you want to make this retreat in its entirety or just part of it?
8. Would it be best for you to make this retreat with another spiritual director?

As with the original interview, I would look for "red flags" and signs that the Spirit is really calling the person. If the person has not completed the retreat, it may be necessary to begin again. Like learning, the return to the retreat can be like a spiral. He or she will discover more, even with the same story and process. Making this retreat again will take a new level of commitment, new skills, and an ever deepening desire to drink from the "living waters," while looking at what prevents the person from doing so. Defenses or resistances that operated the first time may be stronger. On the other hand, the time in-between may have allowed the person to move to a more profound level of self-knowledge. Perhaps the person is now ready to get closer to what he or she is looking for. Although the potential directee may have certain memories or expectations of the retreat from their past experience, it is important to emphasize that this is a new moment, open to the unknowns and the surprises. It is always a challenge to return to something familiar with an open mind and heart.

In order to keep the retreat "fresh," it may not be best to review the journal of the previous experience before this retreat. This review may be appropriate for later in the retreat. For the first meditation have the directees write a "spiritual journey update"—that is, what has happened since the last retreat. To allow for more spontaneity, responsibility, and vitality, new approaches to the same material are encouraged—e.g., spending in-depth time on the *Lectio Divina* with John 4, adding their own questions to some of the journal sections, writing their own **Directee's Prayer**, listening for **Jesus' Response** on a daily basis, reading appropriate books listed in the bibiliography, trying some of the art or music forms of meditation that they did not use the first time. Perhaps other media or resources are appropriate for enhancing their experience. You may find sections of the Spirituality of the Retreat (Chapter 8) or the Psychology of the Retreat (Chapter 9) helpful in clarifying the inner stirrings of your directees.

Megan McKenna in her book *Not Counting Women and Children: Neglected Stories from the Bible* suggests a way of processing the story of the Samaritan woman as a whole. The questions below may be used as a preparation for a return to the retreat or may be sprinkled throughout the retreat. She emphasizes that scripture is meant to bring about unity, community, balance, wholeness, harmony and peace. These goals imply constant conversion; and conversion involves dialogue and interaction with others (i.e., spiritual director, colleagues, spouse, groups). Even more boldly she insists: "All interpretations [of scripture] must push toward reconciliation, forgiveness, restoration, justice, and mercy in their decisions and actions. They must be interpreted so that we are told to bend, to submit, to learn discipline, to obey, to let go of our ways of doing things, to compromise, and to know when something is important and crucial to stick to and when just to let go and let ourselves be reformed and refashioned" (McKenna, p. 224). You may find ways of adapting these suggested questions (McKenna, p. 225):

1. *What does the scripture make you feel?*
2. *Who is in the text? Where? When? What is happening?*
3. *Is there anything in the passage that makes you nervous, bothers, or upsets you? (This is a conversion question. Keep in mind that conversion usually starts at the edge of our awareness and acceptance and that change usually makes us uneasy.)*
4. *What are you going to do as an individual to make this passage come true in your present life? (Be specific and ask your community for insight.)*
5. *By baptism and confirmation we are called to be prophets. Trying to use prophetic language, what is this passage saying about justice, peace, and the poor?*
6. *What are we, as a community, going to do to make this passage come true now and in our lives, parish and community? (Start simply, be specific and act. One response is to practice together works of mercy; the practice of hands-on-justice often leads to more work for justice.)*
7. *What in this passage gives you hope and joy?*

If directees are picking up the retreat where they left off or taking just one section of the meditations, a review of the previous retreat may help them capture the flow and the "mindset." The decision to begin again, to take up the retreat where they left off, or to take only one segment of the retreat is a joint one between the directors and directees.

If the directees still possess their supplementary handouts, you may want to ask them to list them for you. This list serves two functions. Firstly, when you want them to use what they already have, that knowledge saves you from duplicating another copy. Secondly, once you know what they have already processed, you may want to choose alternatives. For this new retreat they will create a journal notebook to hold the journal responses to the meditations and the supplementary materials.

At the end of the retreat, an analysis of the two retreat experiences may be significant. Ask them to re-read their former journal in-depth. They may wish to underline (colored pencil or felt pen) what strikes them now and why, to write down their feelings as they read it. Who is the person that emerged from that experience? Then, invite them to compare and contrast the two experiences in light of the growth that has happened, new insights and continuing concerns. Who have I become now?

Be careful that they do not use you or the structure of this retreat as a substitution for the adventure of true spiritual growth. This retreat aims at giving them the confidence, freedom, and resources in following the Spirit of Jesus—living an authentic life within and responding to the mission in community that is uniquely theirs.

As the director, you, too, have to foster an attitude in yourself of starting afresh. Even if the directees bring unresolved issues from the last experience, you would listen to what they say and how they respond to the questions now. If they make reference to the past retreat, respond to what they are saying about it now. As usual, follow their lead and where Jesus (and the retreat) is taking them. Should the second retreat be made with the same director and directee, remind the directee that both of you have changed. The director-directee relationship has to be re-established with "new" people.

References

- Asselin, David T., S.J., "Notes on Adapting the Exercises of St. Ignatius," David Fleming S.J., ed., *Notes on the Spiritual Exercises of St. Ignatius of Loyola*
- Au, Wilke, *The Enduring Heart: Spirituality for the Long Haul*
- McKenna, Megan, *Not Counting Women and Children: Neglected Stories from the Bible*

Part III

Essential Background

7

Jesus as Spiritual Director:
What Does He Model about the Relationship between
Director and Directee?

One of the dynamics of the longest dialogue recorded in the Gospels is that of a spiritual director in conversation with a directee. This may be why meditating on this particular story is so powerful and transforming. This section quotes much of the research in the thesis of Almita Bey-Carrión found on pages 44–70.

Definition of Spiritual Direction

In her thesis, Almita notices a correlation between her experience as a spiritual director and how Jesus' conversation with the Samaritan woman progresses: "... in looking and listening carefully to Jesus' dialogue with the Samaritan woman, a clear and helpful criteria emerges toward determining what constitutes the relationship of director and directee. Furthermore, reading this story from the focus of spiritual direction gives an understanding of the dynamics of such a relationship."

First, consider the definition of spiritual direction. Almita continues, "Spiritual direction is the ministry of being a *listening presence* to another while at the same time helping the directee to discern the word of God in his or her life. The spiritual director (or friend on the journey through life to God) listens to the directee with love, acceptance, compassion, and understanding. The directee listens to the spiritual director with trust, openness, and faith in the director's ability to guide. Both listen to God attentively, deeply, and with the humility that is born of a receptive disposition before our God who calls us by name.

"In direction the directees cultivate their awareness of a self-communicating God who is ever calling them forth from the tomb of whatever remains unresolved in their life or keeps them less than they really can be. As this occurs, they can know true freedom and the fulfilling joy that comes with naming and living out their best response to God's love for them.

"The spiritual director is an accepting, challenging presence who holds high the pursuit of truth like a beacon, affirming that the achievement of the directee's potential can become a reality to be lived in the present moment rather than in some future time that is locked up in contingencies. Spiritual direction is a relationship of listening-in-prayer—a kind of prayer that permeates and arises from all experiences of human life."

Jesus' Desire for Relationship

Almita sees that definition fleshed out in the story of the Samaritan woman. "As the story opens, the first thing we notice about Jesus is his willingness to extend himself in order to be available to the Samaritan woman (John 4:4). His motivation to take a longer route from Judea to Galilee (v. 3) arose from his driving desire to fulfill his Father's will of offering salvation to all who would believe in him. Spiritual directors must be individuals in whom this same willingness to extend themselves for another resides. Spiritual directors have been called by God to be vital, life-giving channels of God's grace and everlasting love. For it is God's initiative of love that is the foundation on which all spiritual direction builds. Spiritual direction attempts to uncover the 'already there' initiative of God's love in the life of the directee. It is with this awareness in mind that spiritual directors welcome directees and take them into their heart.

"Verse 6 declares that 'Jesus was tired from his journey.' People seeking spiritual growth enter spiritual direction perhaps not realizing how God is pursuing them. This may be as obvious as the need to change a long-standing behavior or as subtle as needing to hear and understand that still, quiet inner voice that has been wanting to get their attention. The purpose of this pursuit is always the further uncovering of their most authentic identity. Whatever that identity may be and however it may be disguised, denied or buried, spiritual direction creates a space in which God has our attention in a very focused way." This dynamic of God's pursuit of a soul is accurately described in Francis Thompson's poem, "The Hound of Heaven," in which God quietly but relentlessly pursues the poet who keeps fleeing God and hoping to find shelter, contentment and love elsewhere.

"From a purely human standpoint, Jesus' weariness is easy to identify with, for who among us does not hold back something of ourselves from God? Spiritual directors understand that whenever someone begins spiritual direction what he or she perceives as a beginning is probably better understood as part of a continuum in the history of God's loving pursuit and longing for this person. What the directee has either tenaciously or unintentionally held on to, held back, or simply not surrendered will manifest itself sooner or later in spiritual direction. It is this *something* that has become a barrier to the relationship God seeks with the directee."

Almita emphasizes, "Spiritual directors have as their central task the facilitation of this relationship between God and their directees. They help directees experience and respond to God's action in their life. Fostering this discovery is the primary function of a spiritual director. Spiritual direction's first concern is helping individuals to place themselves before God who will communicate God's self to them in order to make them free.

"An important fact that could easily be missed is that Jesus is already sitting there at the well when the Samaritan woman approaches (v. 7). How artfully the evangelist paints this word picture of God's initiative of love in the life of this woman.

"On the other hand, the Samaritan woman comes of her own free will to where Jesus sits. She could have easily turned around and decided to come to the well when this stranger was gone. So too, directees must come in the same way to spiritual direction—that is, freely, knowing Jesus is waiting there for them though having no way of knowing what the outcome of this encounter will be. The Samaritan woman did not turn away from the possibility of engaging in conversation with Jesus, though she must have been surprised that he even spoke to her. Entering into dialogue with God is what spiritual directors help directees do; it is the focus of spiritual direction.

"This initial scene brings up fundamental questions regarding the dynamic of spiritual direction: Do we believe in a God who actually does communicate with us corporately and individually? Do we believe that God can be met personally? If we do believe this, where do people meet this God? Ultimately, we believe, that people meet God in their own experience, whether that experience occurs with a community, with one or two others, or alone, as in this Gospel story.

"Continuing with verse 7, Jesus asks the woman for a drink. He is thirsty, but as the story develops we realize that the thirst Jesus brings to the well that afternoon is not only his physical thirst but also his spiritual thirst to bring this woman to believe in him and to offer her the 'living water' that only he can give.

"What usually brings persons to spiritual direction is a yearning for a deeper relationship with God. The encounter that is experienced in spiritual direction takes place in their relationship with God. Directees must become keenly aware of God's love for them and of God's personal call that seeks a response from them. The response may demand that directees be led to uncharted, unthinkable places but this is always a response to God's word heard in the individual directee's heart."

Awareness of Woundedness

Almita observes that many times the sinfulness, weakness and woundedness of the person arises in spiritual direction: "As directees progress in spiritual direction through a slow, often painful process of coming to self-knowledge through prayer and dialogue with the director, they come to experience just how ardently Jesus thirsts for their complete surrender to his love. It would be well to keep this spoken request of Jesus in mind, to allow Jesus to say this to every person who enters spiritual direction: 'Give me a drink; quench my thirst for you.' People would have no need for the ministry of spiritual direction if they had already responded fully to that request Jesus asked one unsuspecting woman so long ago and continues to ask each person today.

"But see what happens. The woman protests by giving reasons why Jesus should not even be speaking to her, much less ask her for a drink (v. 9): she is a Samaritan (loathed by the Jews) and she is a woman, meaning that her culture extends her little respect or dignity. At this point in the narrative the Samaritan woman can respond to this Jewish man only from her wounded self-esteem and feelings of unworthiness before him…. The Samaritan woman understands her identity as being a distancing factor. It is not a big leap to realize that this all-too-pervasive human wound also keeps her from her deepest identity before God as well. Her true identity is buried under the weight of believing she is somehow innately deficient because she is a Samaritan and a woman.

"What this self-description of the Samaritan woman tells us about spiritual direction is that directees come to the ministry of spiritual direction wounded in some way…. This is not to say that the wound is always readily or easily discerned. It usually comes across as feelings or statements of inadequacy, deficiency, failure, acute embarrassment or disgust about the way they behave, react, or respond to situations. It may reveal itself in feelings of being stupid, less than perfect, or not as good as others. The shame or woundedness isolates some part of these directees from others and from themselves. Or perhaps they remain in denial in order to insulate themselves and so are not in touch with reality. Directees rarely enter into spiritual direction with this awareness. However, Jesus is present with this knowledge of the beloved ones and he comes with his healing power to minister to directees as their story unfolds. Spiritual direction, as Jesus who is the true director does it, brings about a liberation for directees. A spiritual director needs to be sensitive to their directees' unhealed woundedness and resulting vulnerability. It's important to love directees as they are in their place in life just as Jesus loved the Samaritan woman and every other person in the Gospels.

"As we see in verse 10, Jesus completely ignores the Samaritan woman's protests. Nothing about her is repulsive to Jesus nor does anything from his cultural background compel him from entering into dialogue with her. This same Jesus, so eager for a personal encounter, awaits us in spiritual direction."

God's Gift

"When Jesus says, 'If only you recognized God's gift…' (v. 10), he refers to himself and to the 'living water' he wants to give the Samaritan woman. It is this very gift that God extends in spiritual direction: Jesus and his 'living water,' which quench all human thirst in an everlasting and eternal way. Yet like any gift, it can be accepted or rejected. It takes a tremendous leap of faith and a radical trust to re-orient one's life in such a way that Jesus, as the source and giver of this 'living water,' becomes the center from which we live every aspect of our lives. Thomas Merton spoke of 'pneumatized' or 'spirit-filled' persons as being the subjects of Christian spiritual direction who undertake radical changes in their manner of being, seeing and living. Jesus is passionately interested in bringing these changes about. This mystery, however, is hidden and needs to be seen and heard in a new way that totally re-orientates one's life towards a new goal."

Almita notes, "Spiritual direction does not hold out the illusion that we are in direction to become perfect. But spiritual direction does say that we can, through persistent prayer and perseverance, make incredible progress in our spiritual quest. Our deepest desires and prayers are heard and answered by God in the way that is best for us. Spiritual direction is a movement from our inner darkness toward the light of God's truth and love. John, in his Gospel and in his story of the Samaritan woman, reminds us of our blindness that prevents us from recognizing the light even when it is in our midst. It is a further task of spiritual direction to aid in the removal of this blindness.

"More than any other phrase in this story, this synthesizes best what is most needed in the pursuit of the spiritual life: 'If only you recognized God's gift' (v. 10). All is gift, if we only have that degree of openness and vulnerability to acknowledge this at every moment. God is ever revealing God's own self as gift. But our perceptions are narrow and controlled by our personal history and how our past experiences have informed and formed us, rightly or wrongly.

"Directees need to pray earnestly for the Lord's self-revelation. However, they may be threatened by newness and strangeness, seeing only what they want to see or what their perceptual and cognitive structures allow them to see. In spiritual direction directees are invited to let God be God. They need to be open to surprise and newness and to try to let their responses be elicited by the reality of God.

"Spiritual direction offers the gift of a deepened relationship with God. Yet how often and in how many ways do we resist this gift—though we say we desire this most of all! Perhaps our resistance is fueled by the fear of letting go of control and of our own perception of reality. At some point directees need to hear Jesus say to them, 'If only you recognized God's gift,' and then be willing to spend time in reflective prayer in order to determine just how this gift is being offered at this time in their life. Jesus comes bearing himself as the One who can satisfy our deepest needs and desires.

"Jesus is the 'living water' that becomes a fountain within us with the promise that 'whoever drinks the water I give… will never be thirsty' (vv. 10, 14). Like the Samaritan woman, directees look to persons or things outside themselves to be the answer to whatever seems to be lacking in their lives. Sooner or later they are confronted with the cold fact that all such pursuits are in vain and have wounded them somehow. The experience of being in spiritual direction, ideally, is an experience of having unearthed in some way the trapped fountain of 'living water' that is found within. They see that their deepest thirst, which may have been unnamed or unrecognized, is for God. Ultimately, fulfillment is found only in striving for God and the things of God, living for God first and foremost, and doing God's will. If this is our fundamental life aim and focus then our deepest thirst will indeed be quenched as Jesus promises in this discourse."

Almita insists that each person has to go at his or her own pace: "Helping a person discover this truth personally requires loving patience on the part of the director as well as an abiding respect for the individual's own rate of spiritual growth. Some directees seem to spiral up the spiritual trellis like a rapidly growing vine, while others grow in a more slow-spreading fashion. Notice how respectful Jesus is of the Samaritan woman's spiritual state. He does not force upon her what she obviously is not spiritually developed enough to realize or understand. A spiritual director needs to trust that the directee will come to truths when he or she is ready to respond to the challenges and demands of such a discovery. Directors must always keep foremost in their mind that the Holy Spirit, who is the Spirit of truth, is guiding, leading, and directing the directee's soul in the manner most conducive to one's individual level of spiritual maturity and awareness."

Encounter with Unconditional Love

"In the next section of our unfolding story, Jesus very tactfully prepares the Samaritan woman for a full encounter with his unconditional love for her (vv. 16–18). It is crucial that the spiritual director be a powerful presence of this same love that accepts a person without judgment or condemnation. Without such an experience of unconditional love and acceptance there is little hope for inner healing. The following paragraph taken from Volume 23 of *Studies in Passionist History and Spirituality* (p. 11) describes the difference Jesus' way of dealing with the Samaritan woman made in her life:

> *Jesus did not come into the world to announce that in the beginning there was an offended God and a guilty man. He came to say that God is with man, very close to all those upon whom life pours out sufferings and privations, very close to those whose peers consider them unworthy sinners. Jesus does not dwell upon culpability, nor does he set before people a black vision of themselves leading them into shame and self-contempt. On the contrary. The Samaritan woman goes her way happily celebrating her meeting with someone who has told her all that she has done. Jesus had told her all that she had done in an entirely different manner so that the result was her feeling healed in life! How many others had been telling her and repeating all that she had done and kept on doing, but, with what a different tone, which loaded her with blame and condemnation.*

Almita continues, "The spiritual director's function is not to be a teacher of morality. Jesus did not assume this role with the Samaritan woman. Rather Jesus accepted her and loved her while at the same time challenging her with intimate knowledge of the truth of her lifestyle as a means of revealing to her who it was speaking to her.

"Facing the raw truth of where our sin, compulsion or weakness lie is never an easy or comfortable experience. It is in prayer and honest reflection that God will seize the opportunity to reveal not only intimate knowledge of us, but more importantly God's unconditional love. In prayer God ceases to be distant and abstract. The communication with God that takes place in prayer and throughout life moves us toward transformation and maturity in Christ. A director does not interfere with the dialogue between the directee and God, but rather facilitates this dialogue, encouraging the directee to listen and respond from the heart."

In their book, *Design for Wholeness*, the authors present a paradigm for dialogue. Using the story of the Samaritan woman as an illustration, the phases include creating a climate where growth and inner healing can take place, seeing others compassionately, responding to people where they are—spiritually, physically, emotionally—risking entering into a relationship that is self-revealing, and confronting in a way that calls to a deeper life (Sofield, pp. 130–131). Before dialogue is possible, Jesus establishes a relationship. This relationship is both nurtured and experienced in prayer.

Almita continues, "In prayer we experience the Lord's reality. Jesus may come as awesome and daunting, or loving and inviting, or enigmatic and disconcerting. However this occurs, the Lord's purpose is to heal and make whole. As this story illustrates, Jesus will be present but waiting for the person to take the step that must be taken if he or she is to become free.

"Directors help to cultivate in directees the disposition of being 'authentic worshipers (who) will worship the Father in Spirit and truth' (vv. 23–24). It is in living according to the Spirit, who is the Spirit of truth, that directees come to real freedom. Only then is the whole person—body, soul and spirit—intentionally directed toward God, toward re-creation in Christ. Ultimately, participation in this process brings hope and energy to the whole created world. At some point and in some way in spiritual direction, directees will personally and profoundly experience the power of Jesus in their lives. It is an experience of understanding 'I who speak to you am he' (v. 26); Jesus is the one who is their Lord and Messiah in the present circumstances of their life. It is furthermore an experience of God's faithfulness to the age-old covenant between God and humanity: 'I will take you as my own... and you shall have me as your God' (Ex. 6:7)."

Another important detail in the story is explained by Almita: "The short statement, 'The woman left her water jar,' (v. 28) is the central challenge to spiritual growth as individuals move through spiritual direction. The water jar can be taken as a metaphor for what needs to be left behind, let go of, or moved on from in the directee's life. This leaving behind and moving on from whatever the 'water jar' represents is the primary focus of the retreat based on this Gospel narrative…. To be able to arrive at authentic living and human wholeness necessitates the serious inner work that spiritual direction offers and the willingness to give one's best response to life's constant call to discover within his or her God-given capacity for transcending all that is not of God."

Change of Heart

Almita notes, "Spiritual direction, as Jesus models it in his encounter with the Samaritan woman, is a call to turn fully to God in this life through a loving, intimate relationship with Jesus Christ. The response to this relationship will determine the degree of inner healing and wholeness that directees realize and enjoy in their life. As the spiritual director in this story, Jesus takes the individual's situation into account so that life change occurs. People experience a change of heart as a result of their conversation with Jesus."

Another word for this kind of change within a directee is *metanoia*. Used several times in Almita's thesis, this word is defined as "a new creation" by Carolyn Gratton in her book, *Guidelines for Spiritual Direction* (p. 31). Although several people in John's Gospel experience a new life by actively turning away from sin, coming to faith in Jesus, and empowered with new behaviors, this Gospel does not actually use the word *metanoia*. Appearing 64 times in the Greek version of the New Testament, this word is more commonly translated as *repentance* or *change of mind*. According to Webster's New Millenium Dictionary of English, it may also refer to spiritual conversion or awakening. These translations, however, do not convey how radical and complete this change may become. In his website, www.eldergraphics, Jim Elder reviews the many definitions of *metanoia* from a historical and biblical perspective. To demonstrate its more radical meaning he uses the metaphor of the metamorphosis of a butterfly. His insight converges with that of the wise spiritual guide, St. Teresa of Avila, who utilizes the silkworm/moth metaphor to illustrate inner healing and other changes that take effect as one draws closer to God. Moreover, Carl Jung, the eminent psychologist, notes the connection between the image of the butterfly and the healing power of the psyche.

Theologically, this radical change is a manifestation of the death and rising of Jesus within us. Our death and rebirth accomplished in the sacrament of baptism infuses our whole life with the dynamics of the Paschal mystery (see Romans 6:1–11). This unfolds through the life of grace and the sacraments. Spiritual direction helps directees notice and respond to Jesus' invitation to the dynamics of spiritual growth.

Almita goes on to say, "Like the Samaritan woman, directees must be encountered by Jesus. They can choose to make the necessary changes in their lives that have become an obstacle to their fullest response to God, leaving behind those 'water jars' that can never quench their deepest thirst. Furthermore, they must live out this change, this new creation they have become, in service to the people of God.

"The conclusion of the story of the Samaritan woman declares that having found the source of 'living water' she now goes forth among her people as a missionary, bringing others to Jesus (v. 28). John's Gospel highlights God's initiative in Christ as he enters the lives and hearts of those who are open to it and they see a new directedness of all that is towards the Father's everlasting love (v. 42).

"The meaning of this change of heart lies in becoming able to love, in being motivated by love, and in becoming a 'fountain of living water' for others as indeed the Samaritan woman ultimately becomes. When a person has been sufficiently freed from anxieties, angers, and other fixations to be able to care about the Lord's love for his people, Jesus will be seen as inviting them to share Jesus' mission, to care for his people as he cares for them, and to travel the journey he travels, sharing both its light and its darkness. The spiritual director has to start as Jesus did with the Samaritan woman by first loving and accepting her before inviting her through his dialogue with her to change the direction of her life."

Almita concludes this section with the statement: "It is clear that Jesus took this woman through a process recognizable today as being what an individual experiences in the ministry of spiritual direction."

References:

- "Living the Passion of Christ", Vol. 23, *Studies in Passionist History and Spirituality*
- Bey-Carrión, Almita, *The Samaritan Woman Directed Retreat*
- Barry, William A., S.J., Connolly, William J., S.J., *The Practice of Spiritual Direction*
- Gratton, Carolyn, *Guidelines for Spiritual Direction*
- Kelsey, Morton T., *Christo-Psychology*
- Sofield, Loughlan, S.T., Juliano, Carroll, S.H.C.J, and Hammett, Rosine, C.S.C., *Design for Wholeness: Dealing With Anger, Learning to Forgive, Building Self-Esteem*
- Welch, John, O.Carm., *Spiritual Pilgrims: Carl Jung and Teresa of Avila*
- www.eldergraphics.com

8

Spirituality: What Spiritualities are Found in this Retreat?

While the Samaritan Woman Directed Retreat stands on its own, it also integrates four fonts of spirituality, primarily—Benedictine, Biblical, Ignatian, and Twelve Step.

Benedictine

Although not familiar with the *LectioDivina* (divine reading) at the time, Almita Bey-Carrión intuitively structured her meditations in a format similar to the *Lectio* (reading), *Meditatio* (meditation), *Oratio* (prayer), and *Contemplatio (*contemplation). Developed by St. Benedict over 1,500 years ago, this form of meditation has been preserved by the Benedictines and rediscovered by many Christians attracted to a deeper spiritual life. Most notably, teachers of contemplative prayer such as Fr. Thomas Keating and Fr. Laurence Freeman promote solid grounding in *Lectio Divina* meditation as a preparation for the gift of contemplation. For the fourth phase, *Contemplatio*, they recommend centering prayer as a tool for quieting the mind.

This style of meditation is not a linear process. During the time of meditation, persons may find themselves returning to earlier phases to enter into them at a more profound level. A spiral may more aptly describe its dynamic.

Thelma Hall, in her book *Too Deep for Words: Rediscovering Lectio Divina*, provides further understanding of the connection between *Lectio Divina* and contemplation (Hall, pp. 9–13). "*Lectio* has sometimes been called a 'methodless method' of prayer. The description alludes to the fact that it is less a learned way of prayer than one which spontaneously 'flows' toward contemplation as its destination, as inevitably as the snow of mountain peaks, melted by the spring sun's warmth, descend through lakes and rivers, and ultimately reach the sea. In a similar way, the progressive levels in *Lectio* are experienced as a unified interior movement which reaches the object of its desire fully only in the final 'contemplation'." She adds, "Far from being an esoteric way of prayer, intended for a sophisticated or chosen few, *Lectio* is in fact such a simple and effortless way of praying via sacred scripture that one wonders how, together with its attendant contemplative dimension, it ever fell into disuse and obscurity."

Hall's definitions of meditation and contemplation are instructive: "The word *meditation* refers to a discursive reasoning process in which words, events, etc., are prayerfully pondered and reflected on with the object of drawing from them some personal meaning or moral. It is basically an activity of the intellect and reason, aided by grace. *Contemplation* is variously described as a 'resting' in God, or a 'loving gaze' upon him, or a 'knowing beyond knowing,' or a 'rapt attention' to God. All such attempts at verbalizing the experience necessarily fail to express the reality, for the simple reason that contemplation transcends the thinking and reasoning of meditation, as well as the emotions and 'feelings' of the affective faculties. It is basically a prayer and experience of pure faith."

The connection between contemplation and action—that is, one's prayer and daily life—is essential. Hall uses an image from Thomas Merton that fits well with the story of the Samaritan woman: "Thomas Merton used an effective image to illustrate this [connection] when he wrote of 'the spring and the stream.' Unless the waters of the spring are living and flow outward, he said the spring becomes only a stagnant pool. And if the stream loses contact with the spring which is its source, it dries up. In this image of Merton's, *contemplation* is the spring of living water, and *action* is the stream that flows out from it to others; it is the same water. But if action is out of touch with an interior source in prayer it eventually becomes arid and barren, and prayer that does not flow into action is cut off from life. This is the integrity of contemplation and action" (Hall, p. 11, cf. John 7:37–39).

Hall continues, "The gift of the Spirit is the 'living water' of contemplation and action, in the Christian whose deepest desire is to be open to the gift, and to allow God's love to be the center and guiding principle of his or her life." Using the story of the Samaritan woman as an example, she reflects: "… in a small town, on an ordinary day, ordinary people through an experiential encounter with Jesus were brought into new life which has changed the world forever."

The Four Phases of Lectio Divina (Hall, pp. 36–56)

In the Samaritan Woman Directed Retreat, directees call upon the Holy Spirit for guidance and read the designated section of John 4 with a listening heart. They are encouraged to note words, phrases, images, feelings, or memories that have energy for them and then to explore freely these before even approaching the rest of the structured meditation. This is the *Lectio*, or reading phase.

In the *Meditatio*, or meditation phase, directees use their mind, imagination, and heart to discover the personal meaning of this passage. The meditations of the retreat facilitate this process. In these, Almita synthesizes biblical exegesis, Jungian psychology, and the dynamic of the Spiritual Exercises of St. Ignatius. Application to the directees' personal life is facilitated by responding to the journal questions. These questions can be answered in writing and in other creative ways. Because sharing of journal responses with the director leads to a broader unfolding of meaning, these are also part of the *Meditatio*. Thus it is important that directees capture in their journal any new insights arising from their conversations with their directors. Over the course of time, the director's guidance and the journal questions invite directees to identify new behaviors to keep them drinking from the "living water" and to discover their unique mission in life. There is a connection between prayer and action.

When ready, directees transition to the *Oratio*, their heart-felt prayer. Although the Directee's Prayer is already written for them (except for the Ninth Meditation), many find their own yearnings, feelings, and questions expressed there. Moreover, they discover that they are not alone in what they are experiencing; someone else seems to understand them intimately. For those just learning to pray in a more spontaneous and personal way, the Directee's Prayer is a good model and template. The directee is encouraged to customize it, if needed.

The *Contemplatio* phase of Almita's meditations takes place at the end of the reading, reflecting, pondering, and praying. In this dialogue with Jesus, *Contemplatio* creates the quiet space to listen for Jesus' Response. This is difficult or awkward for most. Directees are used to a noisy or busy sort of prayer in which they say all the words, do all the thinking, and read all the text. As noted in the "Enhancements to the Meditations," Chapter 4, this part of the retreat takes careful guidance. Those who are quiet enough to hear new insights rising from within and who trust these nudgings enough to respond to them are transformed in surprising ways.

Since *Lectio* is not a linear process, directees may move back and forth through these four phases. As they gain facility with this method, some find themselves in *Contemplatio* at the beginning or in another phase of their meditation rather than at the very end. Resources for finding more in-depth treatment of *Lectio Divina* and centering prayer are found in the bibliography.

Those who have made the retreat are empowered to respond to Jesus' ongoing work in the world. According to Thelma Hall, "There is a whole new and wonderful world of Christian life and ministry opening up to lay people today. A deep life of prayer and 'being for God' can be genuinely compatible with an active and effective Christian presence in this world. To quote Thomas Merton again, the 'Christ who sleeps like dynamite in your paper flesh' has totally identified with all the struggles and pains, frustrations and doubts, disappointments and failures of our life experience, and as well with our human yearning for God and faithful love. He is as intent today on teaching and leading us through his Spirit to follow him in love and total trust, as ever he was in the human life he lived at a specific time in human history. And he continues to 'stand at the door, knocking' until 'one of you hears me calling and opens the door' " (Hall, pp. 12–13).

Biblical

St. Augustine proposes two different "senses of scripture"—literal and spiritual. The "literal" sense emphasizes the inspired author's insight and the community for which he writes. The best writers in biblical exegesis consider the history, archeological evidence, sociology, language, agenda of the author, and genre of literature to get an understanding of the meaning and context of the passage. In Chapter One of her thesis Almita Bey-Carrión summarizes this research on the Gospel of John in general and John 4, in particular (Thesis, pp. 15–43). Some of the exegesis is incorporated into her explanation that follows the short biblical passage for each of the meditations. This chapter contains the most pertinent exegesis for John 4. Her priority, however, is the "spiritual" sense, as reflected in her explanation and the type of journal questions and prayer responses that she created. This sense relied on the guidance of the Holy Spirit, not only for readers during the time the Gospel of John was written but also for the readers today. God's word is still alive and has a message that transcends culture and time. Discerning the spiritual meaning leads to a deeper relationship with God who reaches out in love and calls the hearer to a mission and to a full life in the Spirit.

Biblical Meetings by the Well

Since the well is such a central image in this retreat, it is good to note what the biblical tradition has to say. Those Jewish people who first heard the story of Jesus and the Samaritan woman would bring to it their Hebrew tradition of other significant meetings at a well. Br. John of Taizè in his book, *At the Wellspring: Jesus and the Samaritan Woman*, (Taizè, pp. 6–14) gives examples. In a desert environment, water had to be sought. Digging beneath the sands, a person may discover an underground spring; hence, a well was established. These wells became very important sites for the existence of human societies because they created a place where a whole network of life could arise. Conflict also arose there (cf. Genesis 26:14–15, 18–22).

Jacob's well in John 4 connects with the story of Jacob meeting Rachel. After rolling away the stone from the well, he watered the sheep she was tending. It took him fourteen years of labor before he could marry her. Br. John notes, "According to some traditions, when Jacob rolls away the stone, the water begins to gush forth and becomes a great fountain, so that from that day on there is more than enough water for everybody" (Taizè, p. 9). This version of the story gives a deeper perspective to the Samaritan woman's reply when Jesus promises her "living waters": "Are you greater than our father Jacob…?" (4:12). In other words: Are you going to perform a similar miracle?

Moses, when fleeing Egypt, met seven sisters by the well, one of whom he eventually married (Exodus 2:15–22). There are other details in his story that resonate with the opening of John 4: "When he came to the city Midian… [Moses] sat upon a certain well, and rested himself there after his laborious journey, and the affliction he had been in. It was not far from the city, and the time of the day was noon…."

Thus it is clear that the story of Jesus and the Samaritan woman is in continuity with the patriarchs and Moses. Br. John of Taizè summarizes this trend with his reflection: "Source of life; gathering-place, site of conflict and reconciliation; meeting-place, notably between a man and a woman with a view to marriage; symbol of a God who takes care of his people: the well possesses a density of meaning that makes it a privileged place for understanding the relationship between God and human beings. Jesus profits from this background to transform a simple encounter into a magnificent expression of his message. He reveals in fullness what these human and biblical symbols always wished to communicate" (Taizè, pp. 13– 14).

Key Points in Reading John's Gospel (Thesis, pp. 15–25)

Assimilating all the great themes of the prophets, John uses Jewish images in his presentation of Christ. "I am," a title reserved for God, is found throughout his Gospel. It expresses his understanding of the similar identity of Jesus and the Father. The series of "I am" sayings that connect with great religious symbols—e.g., "I am the bread of life" (John 6:35, 41, 48, 51)—portray Jesus as the fulfillment of all the religious hopes and expectations of humanity.

Almita notes, "John wants to evoke 'belief' or 'faith,' which is expressed clearly. 'These signs have been written that you might believe that Jesus is the Christ, and that believing you might have life in his name' (John 20:30–31). Faith consists in recognizing Jesus as Messiah and Son of God. This faith is another name for love. To have faith is to have life from Jesus; to refuse to have faith is to choose death."

In this story the Samaritans are led from a belief in Jesus as a prophet to a proclamation that he is Savior of the world. Almita observes, "This process suggests that John understands Jesus as transcending all such categories. Furthermore, John does not identify Jesus with the heavenly Son of Man who would come on clouds and judge the world in the future (as in Mark 14:62), but speaks of him as the one who brings judgment now. John wants to make the point that judgment is not some future cosmic event but that it takes place whenever a person encounters the message about Jesus.... A person who believes Jesus' word has eternal life; one who rejects it is already condemned."

John's literary tendency is to focus on individuals, often giving women key roles as disciples: Mary, the mother of Jesus, initiates his ministry at Cana and becomes the "mother" of John's community at the foot of the cross; Mary Magdala announces the resurrection and becomes an apostle to the apostles; Mary and Martha, his close friends, listen to him with deep faith and witness his raising their brother Lazarus from the dead; the Samaritan woman receives the message that he is the Messiah and brings her whole town to faith in him. Some scholars believe that these stories are preserved because of the leadership of women in John's community.

The passage is most concerned with the gradual self-revelation of Jesus. He intends to lead the woman and the Samaritans to faith. Their progress is depicted in verse 42: "It is no longer because of what you said that we believe, for we have heard for ourselves, and we know that this is truly the Savior of the world." Almita comments, "Revelation and faith... (as in John 2:11, 22; 3:11) are the two points of view which dominate the narrative. How revelation makes a stronger and stronger impact and how faith is led upward can be seen from the progression of the woman's faith as expressed in verses 1, 11, 12, 19, 26, 29, and 42. At the climax of Jesus' self-revelation to the woman as he proclaims himself the Messiah (v. 26), the dialogue breaks off; the disciples arrive and so the woman leaves her jug and runs to the village. The intervening scene with the disciples (vv. 31–38) heightens the tension, until the story ends with the men of Sychar confessing their faith in the Savior of the world." Christ is radiant with new majesty in John 4; the source of this radiance is his unity with the One who sent him (v. 34).

According to the sources summarized by Almita, three themes are integrated in this story: the "living water" (vv. 10–14); adoration in "Spirit and truth" (vv. 20–24), and the labors of sowing and the joy of the harvest (vv. 35–38). Utilizing some key passages in the story, she provides exegesis for those who would like a brief biblical analysis. Commentaries provide additional depth for study.

Setting the Scene—Exegesis of John 4:4–6 (Thesis, pp. 25–27)

4:4 "He had to pass through Samaria." "Jesus' passage through Samaria was not a geographic necessity, since other routes were available. Rather, this necessity is in the same category as the one we read about in John 3:14, a necessity to cooperate with God's plan to bring eternal life to all who believe in Jesus...

"The hostility between Jews and Samaritans had its origin during the time of the Judges (cf. Judges 6–9). Samaria had become the capital of Israel after Solomon's kingdom was divided in 922 BC into the Northern Kingdom (Israel) and the Southern Kingdom (Judah). With the destruction of Samaria by the Assyrians in 722 BC, the city becomes half Israelite and half pagan because the Assyrians repopulated Samaria with pagans deported from other parts of the empire (cf. Kings 17:24 ff).

"The Samaritans were not allowed to collaborate in the rebuilding of the Temple [in Jerusalem] when the Jews returned from the Babylonian exile in 537 BC because the Jews held that the Samaritans were a mongrel race, soiled by pagan blood and pagan religion. In time, the rabbis looked upon all Samaritans as unclean—i.e., as people whom Jews could not associate with, or share drinking vessels with, as in this case, without becoming unclean."

4:6 "The site of Jacob's well." "Jesus had gone out of his way, it would seem, to choose the most strikingly unlikely person to receive his first formal statement of mission. The setting for the ensuing discussion between Jesus and the Samaritan woman is very significant. The location of Jacob's well where Jesus sat to rest is well known: it still exists today halfway between Shechem and Askar."

"The hour was about noon." "Literally 'the sixth hour'." The woman's choice of time for coming to the well is unusual; such a choice was done in the morning and evening. Two things are remarkable here: that the woman chooses the hottest hour of the day, and that she does not go to the source at Ain Askar... or Ain Defne at Balata. Lagrange thinks that the spring at Askar did not always flow, or that the woman lived closer to the well of Jacob. Her coming at midday is generally explained by her desire, as a notorious sinner, not to have to meet other women." More recent interpretations of this story do not assume that the isolation of this woman from others was necessarily due to her sinfulness.

Image of "Living Water"—Exegesis of John 4:7–15 (Thesis, pp. 27–32)

4:7 "Give me a drink." "For a Jew facing daily the harsh realities of a dry land and a desert heritage, water meant life. In the Bible water is a symbol for life. Water is necessary for human existence, which is why we find seventeen references to water in this story as opposed to only six references elsewhere in John. The story of the Samaritan woman reveals the new life which is opening to humanity and to all creation in Christ." For the Christian, this new life begins in baptism (see 2 Corinthians 5:14–17, Romans 6:1–11).

Considering it was noon and the long journey Jesus has undertaken, his thirst is understandable. But the fact of his thirst also resonates with the Christian reader in terms of his words, "I thirst," on the cross. From an allegorical association, Jesus is thirsting to bring his work of salvation to completion. On another level, from the perspective of Mother Theresa of Calcutta, Jesus is thirsting for our love, our faith and our participation in his mission.

4: 10 "If only you recognized God's gift." "Jesus utters a mysterious statement which raises the conversation at once to a higher level. It is a revelation which, as in the dialogue with Nicodemus (John 3:3), announces the theme which is to develop in what follows. There is a masterly transition from the outward situation to the inner confrontation of a person with the revealer. If the woman knew the 'gift of God' and the stranger who asks her for a drink of ordinary water, the roles would be exchanged. In characteristic Johannine style, Jesus gives the dialogue a theological turn by means of a mysterious and almost oracular statement that sums up both the content and the purpose of the conversation that is to follow. What Jesus is really saying is: 'If you only recognized God's gift (eternal life) and who it is (the Savior of the world) that is asking you for a drink, you would have asked him instead, and he would have given you the living water of eternal life.' From this standpoint, it is not Jesus who is in need of anything, but the woman; and she is confronted with the one person who can satisfy the deepest needs of humanity."

Almita observes, "What is basic here is the link with the Old Testament imagery. There God is 'the fountain of living water' (Jeremiah 2:13; 17:13). God's worshippers can drink from 'the river of his delights' (Psalm 36:8). Thus, the figurative expression on the lips of Jesus has become for the evangelist a symbol of all that Jesus meant to him. For John, salvation is to be sought only in Jesus, his revelation, and the divine life which he communicates.

"Knowledge of Jesus cannot be separated from knowledge of his gift of 'living water.' The assertion which is meant to give the woman food for thought at the moment and to provoke her to further questions, also becomes a word of revelation for later believers. It urges them to recognize the true gift of God and its only giver, or again, to recognize who speaks the word of God and to ask him for his gifts."

4:11 "Living water." "As in John 3:5 ff where Nicodemus misunderstands Jesus' words about being 'born anew,' so here the Samaritan woman misunderstands Jesus' words about 'living water.' 'Living water,' like the 'rebirth' of which he spoke to Nicodemus, may be deliberately ambiguous. In its figurative sense the expression comes from the Old Testament (for example Jeremiah 2:13; Zechariah 14:8) and signifies divine life and grace."

4:12 "Are you greater than our father Jacob?" "The question serves the double purpose of identifying the 'water of Judaism' that is being contrasted with Christ and of contributing to the 'Johannine irony'—that is, the pattern of John's Gospel in which people so often assert in a superficial way realities that are true in a much more profound sense. Ironical, too, is the term by which she first addresses him. On her lips the title *kyrie* is nothing more than *sir*, a respectful but ordinary form of address. It is also, however, the word by which Christians testified to their faith in their risen Lord (Philippians 2:9–10). It is this word which she, still uncomprehending, uses after he has explained that the 'water' which he will give not only sustains life but is itself the very source of everlasting life. This water, of course, is Jesus himself. John also would expect his Christian reader to think of baptism, which has already been brought in so often in these early chapters of his Gospel, truly the water which gives life. The woman is made to speak the truth without realizing it: Jesus is infinitely greater than Jacob."

4:14 "The water I give…" "The water Jesus is offering is able to quench thirst forever; it becomes a source which flows from within a person; the water springs up. In John 6:32ff and 48 ff the image of bread completes that of water and both are used together in 6:35: 'He who comes to me shall not hunger, and he who believes in me shall never thirst.' Thus the Johannine Jesus takes up this imagery, but in relating it to himself as the present revealer and savior, gives it a new and deeper meaning. He is already giving the water of salvation and the bread of eternal life to all who believe in him. Jesus' gift takes in and penetrates the whole person. All Jesus' gifts become for his believers forces which abide and work within them." Again there is a foreshadowing of the sacramental gifts—Eucharistic bread and baptismal waters.

Almita's analysis continues, "Finally, Jesus affirms that this source flows unceasingly and unendingly. The water is said to 'spring up, bubble up,' to bring out the supernatural 'vitality' of the divine forces bestowed on humanity. The divine gift brought by Jesus retains its vigor, unthreatened by decay, to remain 'forever,' a Johannine notion which recurs constantly. Hence 'eternal life' here also takes on a futurist tinge (cf. John 3:36b; 1 John 2:25). The synoptic usage still makes itself felt and the eschatological outlook is retained. But the eschatological gift is already given by the revealer at the present moment.

"Jesus' gift of 'living water' has now been adequately described. It is a divine gift brought by Jesus from the heavenly world and given to humanity to quench fully, unfolding its vital powers and continuing to work unfailingly till eternal life. If we ask finally what concrete gift is meant, it does not matter much whether we think of the Holy Spirit (like most Fathers and many modern exegetes) or divine life, since for John both are intimately connected. The Spirit is the creator of life (John 6:63a), and hence Jesus, who communicates eternal life, is described as possessing the Spirit (John 12:32 ff; 3:34), baptizing with the Spirit (John 1:33), and pouring out streams of 'living water.' But believers are also said to 'receive' the Spirit (John 7:39, cf. 14:17, 20:22, 2 John 2:27, 3:23, 4:13). It is also possible to explain it as revelation or the words of Jesus, since it is through the words of the revealer that the Spirit and life come to believers (John 5:24; 6:63, 68; 8:51)."

4:15 "Give me this water, sir, so that I shall not grow thirsty and have to keep coming here to draw water." "Like Nicodemus (John 3:9), the woman continues to misunderstand, and asks for the magic water which is to quench all thirst so that she can be free from the need of fetching water. It seems as though Jesus' efforts have been in vain."

Moment of Truth—Exegesis of John 4:16–26 (Thesis, pp. 32–39)

4:16 "Go call your husband." "As he had done before in the conversation with Nathanael (cf. John 1:45–51), Jesus now introduces an apparently irrelevant topic whose purpose is to show that he is possessed of mysterious knowledge. The woman did not expect to have the literal truth of her reply revealed so bluntly; doubtless she answered as she did simply to put an end to a somewhat strange and potentially embarrassing conversation. Now she begins to realize that this is not an ordinary Jew talking to her; she confesses that he must be a <u>prophet</u>.

"Jesus' efforts are not primarily directed at bringing the woman to abandon her sinful way of life. He is trying to make her more receptive to revelation, to lead her to believe in him (cf. vv. 19, 26, 29), which will also bring about a decisive change in her way of life (cf. John 3:21).

"When the Samaritan woman answers evasively that she has no husband, Jesus shows her how well he knows the story of her life. The Jews held that a woman could only marry twice, or three times at most. Though not bound by the laws of the Jews, in general, the strict views of Orientals on morality may have influenced the Samaritans to consider frequent re-marriage as dishonorable and illegitimate. Verse 29 supposes further that the woman is aware of her guilt and of the low opinion which her Samaritan community has of her." Psychologically, Brother John of Taizè observes:

> The text tells us that the woman has had relations with a series of men, none of which was definitive. It is fairly evident that someone who constantly changes partner in this way is searching for something, something that they do not find. This kind of repetition witnesses to a frustration, a basic lack which is unable to be filled. Our psychologists would be happy to inform us that when we perform the same acts over and over again only to find ourselves inevitably dissatisfied at the end, it is time to stop and think things over. Such and obsession leads nowhere; to find what we are looking for, we need to break the circle and move to another level (Taizè, pp. 54–55).

In addition, some exegetes interpret the five husbands in the life of the Samaritan woman as a metaphor for the many gods the Samaritans have worshipped over the centuries (cf. Taizè, p. 54 "… the woman with her five husbands would be a symbol of the Samaritan nation, called by Jesus to give up its idolatry and to return to the God of Israel in order to receive the living water.") Another explanation of her life of constant remarriage may be the deaths of each of her husbands. Since a woman would not have survived economically without a husband or relative taking her in, Jewish law stated that the next of kin was obligated to marry her (levirate marriage). The Samaritans may have had a similar practice. Furthermore, since misfortune is many times interpreted as a punishment from God for sinfulness (cf. story of man born blind, John 9:2–3, 34), no doubt her marital history may have taken its toll on her and her standing in community.

4:19 "You are a prophet." "Samaritan tradition expects 'the prophet' to uncover lost Temple vessels and to vindicate its own tradition of worship. This worship does not take place in Jerusalem but on Mt. Gerizim, which they took to be the location of Jacob's heavenly vision in Genesis 28:16–18. The woman's words may be interpreted as a challenge. Jesus is indeed a prophet, but in a way that far transcends her present understanding."

4:21 "An hour is coming." References to Jesus' "hour" occur often throughout the Gospel of John. Jesus constantly moves toward his hour of return to the Father. In this story Jesus says: "An hour is coming and is already here." The prophetic word about an era that will dawn in a distant future is already present. The works and words of Jesus are already the first fruits of that messianic age. Worship of God will not be tied to the Temple, shrines, or other designated holy places.

Almita goes on to say, "Then—which means from now on—the Samaritans will also pray to the 'Father'—that is, to God as revealed to them by Jesus, and the old shrines will not matter. This prophetic word with which Jesus turns to the woman, with a plea for confidence contains a consoling promise for the Samaritans who have suffered so much contempt from the Jews."

"Woman." Br. John of Taizè reminds us that Jesus uses the word *woman* as a title of respect (cf. John 2:4, 20:13, 15). Moreover, the use of this word indicates that Jesus speaks not only to one individual but also to humanity as a whole, seen as God's partner (cf. Jeremiah 31:15; Hosea 3:1, Zephaniah 3:14; Isaiah 66:7 ff; Taizè, pp. 58–59).

4:22 "Salvation is from the Jews." cf. Ps. 76:1 " 'In Judah God is known.' The Jews against whom Jesus speaks harshly really refers to that section of the Jewish people that is hostile to Jesus, and especially to their rulers. Here the term refers to the whole Jewish people. This line is a clear indication that the Johannine attitude to the Jews cloaks neither anti-Semitism of the modern variety nor a view that rejects the spiritual heritage of Judaism."

4:23 "An hour is coming." "This means that in Jesus the type of perfect worship sought by the Father is already present. When we contrast this with v. 21, we find in John the same eschatological tension that is apparent in the Synoptic references to the kingdom—it is future, and yet it is at hand. The idea seems to be that the one is present who, at the hour of glorification, will render possible adoration in Spirit by his gift of the Spirit.

"Jesus uses the term 'Father,' not just because it is his usual way of speaking of God in the fourth Gospel, but because he is describing the new relationship of the true adorer to God (cf. John 1:12; 3:5 ff; 1 John 3:3:1 ff). The Johannine Jesus often speaks of 'God,' but here he is inviting all who seek God to an unheard-of intimacy with the 'Father.' After the dialogue with Nicodemus, it is easy to understand that the true adorers in 'Spirit and truth' are those who are 'born of the Spirit' (cf. John 3:3–8). Of themselves, humankind can have no access to God and God's heavenly realm (cf. John 3:31); and if persons are to pray effectively, they must also be enabled to do so by God, by being filled with God's Spirit. In true worship there is an encounter with God for which God must make persons capable by grace."

4:24 "In Spirit and truth." "This is not an essential definition of God, but a description of God's dealing with humanity; it means that God gives the Spirit (John 14:16) which begets them anew. There are two other such descriptions in the Johannine writings: 'God is light' (I John 1:15) and 'God is love' (1 John 4:8). These too refer to the God who acts; God gives the Son who is the <u>light</u> of the world (John 3:19; 8:12, 9:5) as a sign of God's <u>love</u> (John 3:16)."

Almita summarizes, "If a person is to adore God 'in Spirit and truth,' then he or she must first be filled and penetrated by the Spirit of God. This is fully and effectively true of believers in Christ since their birth from God in baptism, where they receive power to become children of God (John 1:12 ff; 1 John 3:1ff), are born 'from above' through the Spirit of God (3:3, 5 ff) and are thus enabled to lead a holy, indeed a sinless life which shows itself in love (1 John 2:29; 3:9; 4:7; 5:1, 18). This immediate eschatological gift of the Spirit has come about through Jesus Christ (John 1:17). Hence true adoration in the Spirit is only possible in union with Christ. The worship offered in Spirit and truth is performed by a community of believers. The true adorers are not individualists but God's flock, gathered into one by the Son of God (cf. John 4:37 ff; 10:1–18, 26–29) and continuing to gather to itself all the scattered children of God (cf. John 10:16; 11:52). As the New Testament people of God, it is not subject to the limitations imposed by the history of salvation on the ancient Temple of Jerusalem, whose rites it replaces by worship in Spirit and truth founded on Christ. In Christ there is not difference between Jews, Samaritans and Gentiles.

"Adorers whom the Father wants and seeks implies that the woman must allow God to find her—that is, by responding to Jesus who is speaking to her. Having laid bare her sinful life, Jesus wishes her to accept God's pardon from him and to serve the Father with a pure heart, in Spirit and truth. For this she must believe in Jesus, the revealer and savior. Thus the dialogue culminates in the self-revelation of Jesus as Messiah.

"To be born merely from the 'flesh' is to remain a prisoner of the world of the flesh which is doomed to perish, to be deprived of access to the higher realm of the Spirit which is divine and heavenly. There is a need of a new creation, which can only be brought about by God's power, if a person is to be raised up to meet God and to belong to God."

4:25 "I know there is a Messiah coming." "The Samaritan woman has not grasped Jesus' revelation, and hopes for the Messiah who will 'tell us everything.' She has failed to understand that Jesus is telling her that the present hour is one of fulfillment, of the coming of him who makes the true adoration of God possible.... But her religious yearnings are sincere; she has also perhaps some intimation of the mystery of Jesus, and this provides him with the occasion of revealing himself to her as the expected Messiah (v. 26). In him she can find the fulfillment of her hopes, and the Samaritans along with her."

The Samaritans, who accepted only the Pentateuch of the Hebrew Scriptures as inspired, would have been expecting the promised prophet (Deuteronomy 18:15). Almita notes that "Little is known about messianic expectations among the Samaritans, but John here makes clear that Jesus is the fulfillment of whatever the Samaritans expected in the way of the Messiah: 'I who speak to you am he' (v. 26)."

Come and See—Exegesis of John 4:27–42 (Thesis, pp. 39–43)

4:27 "Surprised that Jesus was speaking with a woman." "The astonishment of the disciples is due to the fact that Jesus is talking to a woman. This short comment of the evangelist underlines the reverent attitude of the disciples towards Jesus, and the two questions show the interest which the disciples take in the conversation.... The awe of his friends makes the mystery of the revealer stand out more strongly. The woman comes once more into the picture, as she hurries away to call the other Samaritans."

4:28 "The woman then left her water jar." Almita offers this insight: "John may be insinuating that she had no further use of it, now that she had found the source of living water." Another perspective is that she entrusts her jar to Jesus. Even though our human thirsts are not enough to satisfy us, they have to be honored and dealt with. What seems very ordinary Jesus can transform (cf. changing of water into wine, John 2:6–10). With that gesture, she put down a burden. Notice the speed, freedom and even joy with which she returns to her town."

4:29 "Come and see." This phrase echoes an invitation Jesus extends to the disciples of John the Baptist (John 1:39). From that encounter they believe that they found the Messiah (v. 41b). In John 4:40–42 the experience of spending time with Jesus also led the people of Samaria to belief. The woman becomes the inviter on Jesus' behalf.

"Could this not be the Messiah?" "The woman is full of the idea that she should bring others out to see the mysterious stranger at the well; it would be out of place, therefore, to draw any conclusions as to her own belief. The strongest argument, she feels, is that the stranger knew of her past life, and hence must certainly have prophetic gifts.... The question as to whether the man is the Messiah or not is put more tentatively. It is meant to cause reflection (cf. v. 39), and the reader is thereby reminded of Jesus' self-revelation (v. 26)."

4:31–38 Jesus speaks of missionary work. "The approach of the Samaritans signals a success for the work of Jesus as revealer. Jesus' conversation with his disciples in the meantime clearly has a missionary character and looks beyond the promising 'harvest,' that is at hand to the future mission of the Church. Just as Jesus is now fulfilling the mandate of his Father, so he too sends out his disciples to continue his work (v. 38). In the words addressed to his disciples he depicts the hidden work of the Father and his own visible success as sowing and harvest (vv. 25 ff) and the metaphor of harvest is retained for the later era which he opens up by his earthly work (v. 34).

"The disciples' urging Jesus to eat leads to his speaking of the food which consists of doing his Father's will (vv. 31–34); this is what makes him look at the harvest at hand (vv. 31–34); and then take in the later missionary work of his disciples (vv. 37). The 'food' is not in the nature of a gift of God or inner strength given by the Father. It is only a way of describing the great interest which dominates the mind of Jesus and claims him totally; the whole expression 'to have food to eat' becomes a metaphor. Jesus has nothing special to sustain him, as the disciples mistakenly believe, but he must put himself completely at the disposition of his Father. In another way, men and women are called upon to 'eat' and 'drink' in a metaphorical sense, by 'coming to Jesus,' by 'believing' in the 'bread from heaven' (cf. John 6:35, 50, 51a) The whole life of Jesus is centered on and grows out of the effort to do the will of the one who sent him.

"Continuing to speak figuratively, he clearly means himself when he speaks of the 'reaper.' Jesus' 'reward' is simply the joy of the harvest (36c); his life and his work are so completely identified (v. 34) that his only desire is to see the 'harvest.' Jesus gathers the people of God to lead it to the Kingdom of God, and sends out his disciples to help with this work or continue it.

"Who is the sower? The contrast between sower and reaper in v. 37, the co-operation between Jesus and the one who sent him according to v. 34, leaves not option but to think of the Father. As they worked together at the sowing they can now rejoice in common at the harvest. Jesus explains to his disciples what their missionary situation is: since he sent them out, they too may reap; but they must remember that others have labored before them."

4:39–42 The faith of the Samaritans. John draws the themes of these two scenes together. On the word of the Samaritan woman the townspeople believe. Almita's research reveals: "But the completion of the Father's work (v. 34), the harvest of the Samaritans, is to have greater durability; for the townspeople come to believe on Jesus' own word that he is Savior of the world. If our story in John 4, particularly in Scene One, has portrayed the steps by which a soul comes to believe in Jesus, it also portrays the history of the apostolate, for the harvest comes outside of Judea among foreigners. We can scarcely believe that the evangelist did not mean for us to contrast the unsatisfactory faith of the Jews in John 2:23–25 based on a superficial admiration of miracles with the deeper faith of the Samaritans based on the word of Jesus. Nicodemus, the rabbi of Jerusalem, could not understand Jesus' message that God had sent the Son into the world so that the world might be saved through him (John 3:17); yet the peasants of Samaria readily come to know that Jesus is really the Savior of the world."

Ignatian

There are many similarities and yet distinctive differences in the paths to conversion as articulated by Almita Bey-Carrión and St. Ignatius of Loyola. Yet both wrote down what they had discovered so that others may experience a deeper Christian life. This section is based on pp. 79–90 of her thesis.

Stories of Conversion

In his book *New Visions, New Directions*, Fr. Robert J. Hater gives a context for understanding the conversion process:

> *If a person shifts his or her way of thinking and acting in light of new insights coming as a result of a retreat, a painful experience, or a joyous event, he or she can be said to have experienced a new level of conversion. If this happens within a faith context, the person is bound to perceive his or her life more deeply in terms of purpose, relationship to God/Jesus/Church, and responsibilities to other persons and the planet.*
>
> *Often, when conversion happens, four elements are present: (1) personal experience; (2) allowing that experience to encounter a broader environment, including the larger Catholic Christian story; (3) illuminating the experience through the encounter and grounding it in prayer, Scripture, church teaching and history; and (4) responding to the insights gleaned in acts of prayer, service, and celebration. These four elements need not flow sequentially nor be present at all times, and each element can happen whether one is alone or with others.*
>
> *Community is central to conversion. An individual "becomes" in community.... In community God is disclosed; in community, a person is supported and encouraged; in community, personal meaning is most fully revealed.... Although it requires community, personal conversion is always an individual search and ought to be facilitated as such (Hater, p. 50).*

On July 3rd of 1990, Almita Bey-Carrión, a laywoman, wife and grandmother had a life-changing experience as she encountered Jesus through the story of the Samaritan woman. She was still recovering from the devastating effects of emerging memories of her childhood sexual abuse (Thesis, p. 2). The foundation of her retreat, as she experienced it, is the great desire of Jesus to be in relationship with us, gradually revealing himself in "all that makes up our daily and personal life, inviting us to the gift of fullness of life."

In March of 1522 St. Ignatius of Loyola, a layman at the time, had a life-changing experience as he read from the life of Christ and the lives of the saints. He was recuperating from serious cannonball injuries that shattered his legs. On retreat at Manresa and during his pilgrimage to Jerusalem, his inner journey unfolded. At the basis of his *Spiritual Exercises* is the "First Principle and Foundation"—God's initiative and passionate love in the unfolding of creation, our response as creatures who praise God, reverence and serve God, and use of the gifts of God only as they help us grow in our relationship with God and others.

Similarities and Differences

Through the *Nine Meditations* and the *Spiritual Exercises* of St. Ignatius, individuals grow in spiritual freedom, come to desire God in all things and above all things, and learn to live a discerning life. They both rely on imagination—calling images to mind, inserting oneself in the Bible story, and entering into dialogue with Jesus. Both are a form of kataphatic prayer—that is, employing thoughts and images. Like the journal work that is an integral part of the Samaritan Woman Directed Retreat, written responses to various questions within the retreat are suggested by Ignatius. Because these retreats are best made under the guidance of a spiritual director, they can be considered spiritual direction in a more structured format.

In her thesis, Almita sees that the purpose of both retreat methods were similar: "The purpose of the *Spiritual Exercises* is removal of all inordinate desires in order to allow greater union with God, for St. Ignatius of Loyola believed that any inordinate attachment is an obstacle to our movement toward God. The scope of the *Nine Meditations* does not look to remove all inordinate desires, but rather to focus on a particular inner conflict that is blocking our spiritual growth and must be removed. Both retreats are spiritual exercises, meaning they are methods of disposing the soul to rid itself of inordinate attachment, and, after their removal, of seeking and finding the will of God in one's life." Ultimately both retreats aim at helping people discover their deepest identity and destiny. St. Ignatius calls this making an election; Almita calls this discovering a mission.

For both of these retreats to be most effective, the persons making them have to be well disposed. Ignatius writes in his introductory observations to his *Spiritual Exercises* that persons must be able to make the personal effort required (Exx. 1), have a sincere desire to open the self unconditionally to God's gift of Himself [sic.] (Exx. 5), be ready to pray even in times of desolation (Exx. 12–13), be completely open to the director and report all that they experience (Exx. 17), and be desirous of making as much progress as possible (Exx. 20). Because the Samaritan Woman Directed Retreat and the Nineteenth Annotation of the *Spiritual Exercises* are made in the framework of a person's everyday life, the person also has to be able to sustain reflection in the midst of distractions. Almita suggests, "The director needs to ask directees if they feel capable of keeping the retreat frequently in mind and of coming back to it occasionally in all sorts of circumstances. In other words, it is crucial that they be capable of being engrossed with the retreat, becoming familiar with it so to permeate their being."

Unlike the guidance given for doing the *Spiritual Exercises*, Almita states that for the *Nine Meditations* one has to be at least thirty-five years old or older, that is, in the area of mid-life. She goes on to say, "A basic premise of the *Nine Meditations* is that the Samaritan woman was herself in mid-life and a time of reassessment and redirection, and therefore psychologically ready to negotiate some of the issues particular to this phase of life." Almita cautions that careful discernment of the director was important to assess readiness because chronological age does not guarantee the directee's emotional, psychological and spiritual readiness.

The Four Weeks of the Spiritual Exercises of St. Ignatius

Utilizing many Scriptural passages, the *Spiritual Exercises* identify four progressive movements. One of the tasks of the director is to help directees stay within each movement until deemed ready to move on to the next. Discernment requires an awareness of consolation and desolation, and the practice of the daily Examen of Conscience. In the **First Week** of the *Exercises,* the individual encounters sin and evil in the self and in the world and seeks God's mercy and forgiveness. In the **Second Week** directees ponder the mysteries in the life of Christ and are invited to choose the values of Jesus and grow in friendship with him. During this time they begin formulating a resolution ("election") to help them live a more Jesus-centered life and share in his mission.

Based on a profound personal experience in 1965, Fr. Herbert Alphonso, S.J. understood Ignatian "election" as discovering one's personal vocation: "The only thing that would be proportionate to the deep and demanding dynamics of the Exercises would be the taking hold of one's whole and entire life—the totality of it—to turn it over to God. This is what a 'conversion' is in its profound biblical sense—a 'metanoia,' a change of direction. No wonder St. Ignatius spells out the nature and purpose of his Exercises as 'every way of preparing and disposing the soul to rid itself of all inordinate attachments and, after their removal, of *seeking and finding the will of God in the disposition of my life for the salvation of my soul' (Sp. Exs. 1).* In other words , the goal of the Exercises is 'Election,' or the seeking and finding of God's will in *the arrangement or ordering or orientation of my life ...for salvation."* One way to understand this election is one's state of life. But Alphonso proposes that the meaning is more radical: "...in fact, at its deepest level, ... [it] is my unrepeatable uniqueness, the 'name' by which God calls me—that is, my truest or deepest 'self,' my 'Personal Vocation,' as I have termed it." By becoming more free and aware of God's personal design, a person can accept it and live it out "faithfully and generously" (Alphonso, pp. 19-20).

Then, directees stay by Jesus' side as he walks through arrest, torture and death in the **Third Week**. They come to realize that Jesus died for them so that they may live. This week is an opportunity to know the mystery of suffering and find Christ there, to experience the cost of love and discipleship, and to appreciate and accept God's unconditional love for them. In the **Fourth Week**, directees experience a deep abiding joy in knowing that they are redeemed and that Jesus' victory over sin and death can be extended to all. Jesus' joy and desire to be with us is so great that he returned, even after his life in human flesh had been ended.

Joseph Tetlow, S.J. in his handbook, *Choosing Christ in the World,* sees the **Fourth Week** as a culmination of the whole retreat (pp. 226–227). He refers to the final meditation, "The Contemplation for Learning to Love Like God," as a summary of the grace of this retreat: "For Resurrection lies beyond our dreams and vastly beyond our powers. And 'The Contemplation for Learning to Love Like God' takes the exercitant through an experience of the renewed paradigm: God giving me all good gifts and making me gift, God remaining within and behind each and every created being, God working busily to bring salvation to all creatures, God sharing the divine gifts and Self. Everything is God's initiative."

Ignatian Dynamics in this Retreat

Although more loosely structured and less detailed than the *Spiritual Exercises,* the *Nine Meditations* of the Samaritan Woman Directed Retreat have some of the same dynamics of the Ignatian **Four Weeks**. Almita reminds us that in both it is up to the director to "'hear' the growth that is taking place within directees as they work through the retreat and share all that is transpiring there."

Usually it is an experience of "the cross"—that is, suffering—that leads persons to seek out the Samaritan Woman Directed Retreat. Somewhere in their mid-life crisis, they find themselves empty, caught in addiction, compulsions, obsessions, or just plain stuck. Notice in the passage before the beginning of the First Meditation, the jealousy of the religious leaders is implied: "Now when Jesus learned that the Pharisees had heard that he was winning over and baptizing more disciples than John... he left Judea and started back for Galilee again" (John 4:1–3). The growing popularity of Jesus leads them to plot his arrest and death (**Third Week** material).

From the very beginning, the dignity and worth of directees are affirmed by Jesus; he chooses to meet them there at the well because "He had to pass through Samaria," (v. 4). His great desire to be there had a personal cost: "… Jesus, tired by his journey…" (v. 6). Jesus offers her a gift of God, that is, the gift of "living water" that will quench her deepest thirst (vv. 10, 13–14). Thus, the opening of this story establishes the Principle and Foundation of the retreat just as the *Spiritual Exercises* do.

At the same time, Ignatian **First Week** material appears in the journal questions of the First through Fourth Meditations. They invite directees to identify their well, what alienates them from their truest self and others, what gets in the way of a full and free response to God, and the central conflict in their life. Likewise, this is found in Jesus' observation about the woman's five husbands and the present man she is living with (John 4:16–18).

Second Week material appears in the Second through Seventh Meditations. Jesus gradually reveals himself to her as the source of "living water," the prophet, and the Messiah. In the Eighth Meditation, Jesus reflects on the fruitfulness of his ministry by doing the Father's will. Journal questions in the Sixth Meditation invite directees to begin envisioning a resolution (election) and by the Eighth Meditation they have identified their mission, established their goals, and what they need to do to sustain them. What is God's will for them that will bring the new life promised by Jesus? Most essentially, this is a discovery of the personal vocation, a unique response to their faith and relationship with Jesus. The practice of the Examen of Conscience may be recommended to help them stay in the flow of the "living water."

Also in the Eighth Meditation's journal questions, directees face the obstacles and the radical "letting go" (leaving her jar behind, v. 28) necessary for new life to emerge. This is similar to **Third Week** material.

The scripture of the Seventh Meditation reflects the woman's joy of discovery (vv. 29–30), which is **Fourth Week** material. Since she has experienced an inner resurrection, she runs back to her town to tell others about the person who brought about this transformation. Not only do the townspeople respond to her enthusiasm but also they encounter Jesus. Out of their personal experience they proclaim with deep faith, confidence and joy, "we know that this is truly the Savior of the world" (v. 42). The final journal question asks directees to tell what happens to the Samaritan woman next. The correlation between what they imagine and what they have experienced during the retreat is uncanny.

Unique to the Samaritan Woman Directed Retreat is a closing ritual as a way of celebrating endings and beginnings, death and rebirth, **Third and Fourth Week** material. Almita writes, "An optional tenth session is suggested as a way to bring the entire retreat experience to closure. This is in the form of invitation to create a ritual experience as an expression of all that emerged from the retreat as well as the resolutions that have been made. This will be a very powerful and personally significant experience for the directee." Ann Belford Ulanov in her book *Receiving Woman* offers insight into this inner birthing process:

> *The soul must attune itself to the inner other of the spirit and follow its transforming lead. The soul both participates vigorously in the birth act and submissively receives the will and tempo of the "other" as it is brought into the world of personal actions and reactions. The time of this delivery, moreover, whether it be physical birth or a spiritual birth, carries decisive authority. It is time as kairos. From its date all other times are reckoned as "before" or "after." New life has begun. This moment invests all other moments with value. A concrete and particular "other" has come into being (Ulanov, p. 107).*

Recognizing the new birth at this stage in the retreat, Almita observes, "Ending the *Nine Meditations* with a ritual expression of this new life the directee has received is a way of releasing and calling into being with authority the new energy and creativity that he or she now feels. It is a moment of great joy; a truly 'magnificent moment.' The Self, or God-image, is breaking through."

Finally, these two retreats have such a similar dynamic that some of those who have made the Samaritan Woman Directed Retreat have gone on to make the *Spiritual Exercises* of St. Ignatius. They found the former as an excellent preparation for the latter. From my experience, even though I had made several Ignatian retreats (both 8–day and 30–day versions) previous to this retreat, only in the Samaritan Woman Directed Retreat did I discover a <u>core wound</u> out of which all other inordinate attachments had arisen. This was a key revelation for my conversion. However, all the years of the Ignatian retreats may have prepared me for the power and possibilities of the Samaritan Woman Directed Retreat.

Necessary Qualities of the Director

Almita notes similarities in the qualities needed for the director from St. Ignatius Introductory Observations (1–20) and his Presuppositions (22): "Ignatius reminds the director that there is a need to adapt direction to each individual person, always leaving room for the action of the Holy Spirit. The director must help the person to clarify one's experience and to discern. Furthermore, the director assists the person to focus one's whole body-person on the Lord in prayer. Above all, the director is never judgmental, never shocked at what is heard. One does not give homilies or teach or develop one's own insights. The director offers questions to help the directee clarify his or her own experience of God and give information when the person is experiencing a spiritual problem. The director may be called upon to help a particular directee clarify images of God. Most importantly, a good director is patient—giving time for the Holy Spirit to work within the directee. The director never resorts to manipulation or self-seeking. The director is merely an instrument of the Lord."

Critical Guideline

In order to know deeply the power and dynamics of these retreats, both require that the directors make it before they lead others through it. Almita reinforces this guideline as follows: "It is my strong recommendation that prospective directors of these *Nine Meditations* first experience this retreat themselves with their own spiritual directors before attempting to lead someone else through it. This will make possible their clear, integrated understanding of the Gospel account and its concepts on many levels: theologically, exegetically, spiritually, and symbolically. The directee may need guidance in understanding what Jesus means by the 'living water,' since this person will be expected to desire it and ask Jesus for it as a help in resolving whatever inner obstacle has surfaced during his or her retreat. Unless directors have discovered this 'living water' as a source of grace and strength in their own life, they will not be able to help their directees move towards it with trust in what Jesus is offering."

Twelve Step Spirituality

It was 1940, a time of great discontent for Bill W., the founder of Alcoholics Anonymous. At his doorstep appeared the Jesuit priest, Father Ed Dowling. Through their subsequent conversations over twenty years, Ed shared with Bill the similarities between the Spiritual Exercises of St. Ignatius and the Twelve Steps that Bill had identified as necessary for the recovery of an alcoholic. They found that the most effective sponsors, counselors and spiritual directors for persons in recovery were former alcoholics. Experienced in the "wiles" of addictive and obsessive behavior, they possess inside knowledge of the power and dynamics of Twelve Step Spirituality.

Over the years I have noticed how effective this Samaritan Woman Directed Retreat has been for those recovering from addiction, obsessions and compulsions. Essential to the Twelve Steps is honesty. The *Alcoholics Anonymous Big Book* states the situation in the chapter, "How It Works":

> *Rarely have we seen a person fail who has thoroughly followed our path. Those who do not people who cannot or will not completely give themselves to this simple program, usually men and women who are constitutionally incapable of being honest with themselves. They are such unfortunates. They are not at fault; they seem to have been born that way. They are naturally incapable of grasping and developing a manner of living which demands rigorous honesty (AA, p. 58).*

During recovery, the addict shifts from denial of reality to a searching and fearless moral inventory of his or her life. Honesty is tested as this inventory is shared with another. Recovery deepens as the person continues to be honest about one's life and behavior and promptly admit any wrongdoing.

Honesty is critical in the dialogue between Jesus and the Samaritan woman. Only after she was willing to admit her marital situation does the conversation shift. Jesus commends her honesty and begins to reveal himself in more depth. Likewise, this retreat is most effective for those who are ready to move beyond unconsciousness, illusions, stereotypes and denial. Though we may be honest with ourselves, trusting another sufficiently to share our experience is also a challenge. Only those who can take this risk will benefit from the honest feedback from the director.

In addition, the sequence of the story seems to parallel many of the Twelve Steps. Following the interpretation of the steps by Mary E. Mortz, *Overcoming Our Compulsions*, pp. 4–5, are the congruent parts of the Samaritan Woman Directed Retreat:

Step 1: "I admit that I am powerless over life, over others, and over myself. My life has become, in some way, unmanageable. I'm stuck." The well that we discover in this retreat is very deep in our psyche, very entrenched in our habits. We keep returning there. To satisfy her thirst, the Samaritan woman returns to the well daily; she comes alone at midday, not when the other women gather there.

Step 2: "I came to believe that there is a power greater than just myself in this world, here and now. This Higher Power can restore me to a happy, fruitful, whole, and sanely balanced life." We have tried life our way, and Jesus has become tired pursuing us. We look at things from our perspective and keep missing the meaning of his message. We may have even missed who he really is and wants to be for us. Jesus tells the woman that if she knew the gift he was offering she would have asked him for a drink.

Step 3: "I accept to make the decision to surrender, to "let go, and let God" take over my life. I agree to let God care for me, and to cooperate with him." We may "hit the wall" during the retreat, meaning that we suddenly realize where our efforts have brought us. Although we may not be sure what the alternative may be, we are willing to trust Jesus to guide us to a more life-giving place. Like the Samaritan woman we ask to drink from the "living water" he promises.

Steps 4 and 5: "When I am ready and without fear, I accept the challenge to look over my entire life. I review my patterns of feeling, my relationships, my work, my play and my sex life. I look at the harms and the hurts I have experienced, as well as those I have done to others. Then, I share my fourth step insights with another person. I 'confess' them, admitting everything, to someone I trust." As the retreat deepens, we identify our well and the core wound beneath it. We admit this to ourselves, to Jesus and to our spiritual director. When Jesus asks the Samaritan woman to call her husband, she admits she has none. He goes on to acknowledge her history with many men. She does not deny it. Neither does he condemn her. The way he responds to her is an invitation to discover even more truth—truth about her and truth about God, her Higher Power.

Steps 6, 7, 8, 9, 10: "I review Steps One through Five again. I look at my character gifts and defects that have surfaced. I pray for the willingness for God to remove the defects and fill the void that I so fear. I pray for the willingness to use my gifts as God sees fit. I ask God to take away any negative patterns of feeling, responding, thinking, I have that are stumbling blocks for me or others. I prepare a list of anyone and any institutions that I have harmed in any way. I go about the task of expressing sorrow where necessary, and I work to make right the wrongs I have done, if this is possible. Daily I continue to examine my 'conscience' for the good and the not good of my life." Entering into deeper honesty, we notice more and more how the well contaminates our life. The director encourages us to begin visualizing the "living waters" as a replacement for all that we have discovered in our well. Our Higher Power—that is, Jesus who sits by the well—invites us to release what burdens us and to use our gifts differently. As we gradually identify our mission, our goals and strategies for living them, we let go of all that had been holding us back from our truest and deepest Self. Like the Samaritan woman, we let go of our jar, we become free from our negative patterns in order to live life fully. This process takes constant vigilance, since wells of addictions, compulsions or obsessions are cunning, baffling and powerful.

Step 11: "I let God in everyday. I allow space and open the door to an awareness of my Higher Power in my life. I remain open to learning to listen to God, to communicate with God. I allow this divine love to deepen in me and to flow out into all areas of my life." We have been in conversation with one whom we discover to be both prophet and Messiah—powerful, yet personal; revealing, yet accepting. Above all, we discover both intimate dialogue and silent attentiveness as a way of staying in conscious contact with the source of our healing and new life. Likewise, the conversation with Jesus is the source of the Samaritan woman's transformation and enthusiasm. Conversation with Jesus also brings the townspeople to belief and conversion. In the Twelve Step Spirituality conversation with one's sponsor and home group is critical to the recovery process. It is there that one's concrete experience with the Higher Power may first be experienced. The retreat models and develops the conversation from prayer to meditation, from meditation to contemplation.

Step 12: "Having experienced new life and growth, I share my newly found life with others. I find respectful, non-intrusive ways to do this. I practice my newly found 'life habits,' my new principles, in all the aspects of my life." We are sent out to live this new life in our relationship to Jesus and in relationship to a mission we have come to know more clearly during this retreat. We set up a way of processing the graces of the retreat and of supporting the movement forward, one day at a time. In us the Samaritan woman completes her mission—that is, to bring one more person to the source of sanity, freedom, truth, serenity, and love. That source is Jesus.

References:

- Alcoholics Anonymous, *The Big Book*, Fourth Edition, New and Revised
- Alcoholics Anonymous, *Pass it On: The story of Bill Wilson and how the A.A. message reached the world*
- Alphonso, Herbert, S.J., *The Personal Vocation: Transformation in Depth Through the Spiritual Exercises*
- Bergan, Jacqueline Syrup and Schwan, Marie, *Praying with Ignatius of Loyola*
- Bey-Carrión, Almita, *The Samaritan Woman Directed Retreat*
- Charpentier, Etienne, *How to Read the New Testament*
- Crossan, Dominic, O.S.M., *The Gospel of Eternal Life*
- Cowan, Marian, C.S.J. and Futrell, John Carroll, S.J., *The Spiritual Exercises of St. Ignatius of Loyola*
- Cusson, Gilles, S.J., *The Spiritual Exercises Made in Everyday Life*
- Ellis, Peter F., *The Genius of John*
- Hall, Thelma, *Too Deep for Words: Rediscovering Lectio Divina*
- Hater, Robert J., *New Vision, New Directions: Implementing the Catechism of the Catholic Church*
- Mortz, Mary E., *Overcoming Our Compulsion: Using the Twelve Steps and the Enneagram as Spiritual Tools for Life*
- Murdy, Kay, *What Every Catholic Needs To Know About the Bible: A Parish Guide to Scripture*
- Perkins, Pheme, *Reading the New Testament*
- Puhl, Louis, J., *The Spiritual Exercises of St. Ignatius*
- Schnackenburg, Rudolf, *The Gospel According to St. John*
- Schneiders, Sandra M., *Written That You May Believe: Encountering Jesus in the Fourth Gospel*
- Br. John of Taizè, *At the Wellspring: Jesus and the Samaritan Woman*
- Tetlow, Joseph, S.J., *Choosing Christ in the World: Directing the Spiritual Exercises of St. Ignatius of Loyola According to Annotations Eighteen and Nineteen: A Handbook*
- Ulanov, Ann Belford, *Receiving Woman: Studies in the Psychology and Theology of the Feminine*
- Vawter, Bruce, *The Four Gospels*

9

Psychology of the Retreat: How Does a Jungian Approach Enhance this Retreat?

Importance of Psychology (Thesis, pp. 62–70)

Infused within the Samaritan Woman Directed Retreat is psychology, especially as it relates to mid-life. Almita Bey-Carrión proposes in her thesis: "While spiritual direction is not the 'spiritualization' of psychology, this ministry cannot be done… without the inclusion of knowledge from some sources of psychological findings regarding human growth and development. Jesus, the author of human life, could not but bring the fullness of this knowledge to every situation, not least of all to his encounter with the Samaritan woman. It is in this same Gospel of John that we are told that Jesus '… needed no one to give him testimony about human nature' (John 2:25)." John Sanford wrote in a foreword to Hanna Wolff's book, *Jesus the Therapist*, that she sees "deeply into the person and teaching of Jesus of Nazareth, in whom she sees a physician of the soul…[He] was the first great depth psychologist, and even to this day, the most unique. The ego may think it can disregard its spiritual origins, but the soul hungers for a connection to the original well of water from which it once drank" (Wolff, ix).

For men and women negotiating the issues of mid-life, Jungian psychology has much to offer. In Carl Jung's *Collected Works*, is this statement: "Among all my patients in the second half of life—that is to say over thirty-five—there has not been one whose problem in the last resort was not that of finding a religious outlook on life" (Jung, p. 334). For Jung, recovery of religious experience was a "cure" for loss of faith and meaning in life. Religion, rightly understood, has the potential for healing, renewing and transforming a person open to its influence. While religion has the goal of holiness, Jungian psychology insists that holiness includes the wholeness emerging from a process of individuation.

Major Jungian Concepts (Welch, pp. 66–72)

To understand this complex process, a few definitions of terms and Jungian concepts may be helpful. John Welch in his book, *Spiritual Pilgrims: Carl Jung and Teresa of Avila*, explains the basics: "The *psyche* refers to the totality of the personality. It is a spaceless space, an inner cosmos which incorporates all psychic processes, conscious as well as unconscious…. *Consciousness* is that part of the psyche known directly by the individual. It consists of thoughts, memories, and feelings which are present to one's awareness. In relationship to the unconscious, it is the smaller part of the psyche. The *ego* is the center of consciousness since experiences of the outer and inner worlds must pass through the ego in order to be conscious…. It is an island of identity and continuity for the *personality*. A healthy ego-consciousness is an important goal in human development." This last statement is especially true in the first half of life. The *persona* is part of the personality that a person consciously develops and reveals to the outer world. *Superego* includes all the messages received from parents and other authorities in a person's life.

Welsh continues, "The psyche has within its space *energy* or *libido*. Psychic energy moves throughout the space of the psyche and does the work of the personality…. Some of the energy is derived from the instincts, but for the most part energy is the result of experiences. Interaction from the environment generates energy in the psyche…. Fundamental to energy in the psyche is movement…. The principle of opposites is a way of thinking about psychic processes. Movement, even in the outer world, appears to be the result of contending forces, dynamic tension…. The psyche's movement to harmony and wholeness is the balancing of opposites…. Energy which disappears from one part of the psyche will reappear in another part. The psyche is a relatively closed system and, consequently, energy does not escape. For example, many events which made a lasting impression on us are not present in our consciousness but are very much alive in our unconscious…. Similarly, energy in the unconscious may appear in conscious activity. For example, the unconscious effects of a relationship with one person may influence our relationship with a second person. Psychologists speak of this dynamic as transference.

"Another principle of psychic process is the *principle of equilibrium*. The energy represented in polarities will tend toward balance. A movement of harmony and balance persists throughout the psyche. When one pole of a bi-polar situation has received more energy than its opposite, the energy then tends to flow to the neglected pole…. A complete balancing, or stasis, never occurs because new energy is constantly being added as a result of new experiences.

"The *unconscious* refers to those aspects of personality which are not present in the awareness of the individual. The unconscious is the realm of that which is unknown within the psyche… it is the source of materials for the consciousness and has a creative role in the psyche."

Welch notes, "Jung identifies two layers of the unconscious. The layer closer to consciousness he calls the *personal unconscious*…. [It contains] thoughts, memories and feelings which at one time had been conscious… impressions which were never strong enough to become conscious. In general, the personal unconscious develops as a result of personal experiences of the individual who is growing into consciousness. Certain contents in the personal unconscious group together into constellations of energy which Jung called *complexes*…. These complexes act as autonomous little personalities within the psyche. They represent touchy areas which distort reality and have an attraction over the ego. For example, someone with an inferiority complex relates all experiences to that feeling."

Dealing with the Shadow (Welch, pp. 60–61, 119–123)

In the personal unconscious is the *shadow*, that is, the neglected and negative side of one's personality. Disowned qualities, buried desires and emotions dwell here. Welch explains that the shadow, opposing one's conscious identity, "represents the past, the primitive and inferior parts of the self that have not been given the chance to dwell in the light." Though we are not aware of its energies, the shadow can fuel behaviors and feelings that drain and sabotage life. By naming and claiming what is buried in the shadow, one can seek healing and harness these energies for growth and a more "true" self-concept: "The shadow contains not only negative elements and destructive possibilities, but also potential for greater growth and development of the personality.

Jung found that the shadow is ninety percent gold…. Much of what is in the shadow is the unlived life of the individual. This 'positive' aspect of the shadow represents potential which could be tapped, but pressures, fears, or perhaps an unwillingness to take responsibility makes it difficult to 'own' this part of the self." Thus, as Margaret Mead observed, most people live out only five percent of their potential.

Since a person's ego is a strong "gatekeeper," direct revelations from the unconscious are uncommon. As one explores the unconscious, the shadow is most likely the first to be met. In dreams, the shadow appears as a same sex person with qualities opposite of the conscious self-concept (the persona) of the dreamer. Symbolic expressions in story, writing, photographs, art, and music are other ways of gaining access to the shadow. Persistent images connected to feelings and words, identification with certain characters in a story, and analysis of projections can give clues as well. For Jung images from his daily life and dreams indicated the unlived life that was seeking expression in him and led him more deeply into the mystery of his life. Meanings can be gleaned from these by *active imagination* and by *dream amplification*.

However, as Welch observes, the "shadow must be experienced to be truly accepted. When the shadow is merely intellectually acknowledged, it is still being kept away. To feel the repulsiveness of the negative contents of the shadow and to admit that they belong to oneself is a disturbing process." An encounter with the shadow is suggested by the first half of the Samaritan woman retreat when the directee is invited to look into the waters of the deep, dark well. From the Jungian perspective, the image of water represents the unconscious and immersing oneself in water is the symbol of entering the unconscious. Welch claims, "Psychologically, water refers to spirit that has become unconscious. It does not, then, mean a regression to an inferior life but a descent to depths where there is a possibility for nourishment. Healing and new life can be the result of entering these waters. The waters of baptism are certainly meant to symbolize this transformation. The descent is necessary before there can be an ascent."

Many who make the retreat initially react to the discovery of their "well" with disturbance, sorrow, frustration and shock. At times, it takes several sessions for them to accurately identify it and respond to it. This process, however, is a prerequisite for their healing. Welch concludes with a hopeful promise: "Deep waters contain life which is invisible to surface eyes, and on the bottom rest wrecks and treasure for the finding."

Importance of Archetypes (Welch, pp. 73–75)

Welch explains a key concept in Jungian psychology: "The deeper layer of the unconscious Jung calls the *collective unconscious*. This layer differs from the personal unconscious in that its existence does not depend upon personal experience. The contents of the collective unconscious have never been conscious and are the result of heredity and evolution…. Within the collective unconscious are pre-existent forms which Jung called *archetypes*. The archetypes are primordial images common to all humankind…. Jung arrived at the theory of archetypes as he discovered common patterns and themes in dreams of present day patients as well as in the fairytales and mythology of history. The specifics of images and stories differed according to individuals and cultures but the underlying patterns of meaning were the same. Such studies led him to assume a transpersonal level of psyche which was fundamental for human development.

"Jung named many of the archetypes found within the collective unconscious such as birth, rebirth, death, the journey of the hero, God, the wise old man, the earth mother, and objects of nature such as sun and moon. These and other images represent typical experiences and motifs in life and the psyche has an inherited tendency to respond to these situations and motifs with typical responses. The archetypes provide patterns of meaning and guide growth for the developing personality. A person's conscious experience is what gives the archetype specific content." According to John R. Yungblut, in his book, *The Gentle Art of Spiritual Guidance*, archetypes carry specific messages through fantasies and dreams which can represent the voice of God within.

Archetypes become known in the consciousness as a *symbol*. For Jung a symbol is a best possible expression for something that is really unknown. Welch explains, "It transforms energy in the unconscious into an equivalent conscious form. The symbol is not consciously created but is a spontaneous formation out of the unconscious. This 'image' comes forth pregnant with meaning [if a person is open to symbolic interpretations]. It provides partial understanding but, as symbol, it points to what cannot be understood. Images… become symbols when they give a specific content to the archetype. The image then becomes the route to the energy of the archetype, making that energy available for the development of consciousness and the growth of the personality as a whole." Examples of archetypes of self—king, savior, prophet, circle, square, cross—appear in myths, fairy tales, and the imagination. Important to note in the story of the Samaritan woman is the revelation of Jesus as prophet and savior. As such, he becomes the "route" to the development of her consciousness and growth; that is also true for the directee. See section on mandalas for a discussion of the circle archetype (p. 95).

Encounter with the Feminine Archetype (Thesis pp. 71–78)

One of the most important psychic qualities to integrate into one's personality is what Jung calls the "deep feminine." It is also present in the psyche in the archetype of the *anima*. In *The Great Mother*, Eric Neumann noted two characters within the feminine archetype. The *elementary feminine* gives birth, nourishes and surrounds; it makes secure and asks for loyalty. On the other hand, the *transforming character of the feminine* drives toward motion and change; it demands relationship, risk, and growth. The latter is less common (Neumann, pp. 24 ff).

Men come to know their feminine side as they become aware of projections in their relationships with women. Because archetypes reside in the collective unconscious, a mythic reading of the story of the Samaritan woman can facilitate the discovery and value of the feminine. Almita observes that the feminine is a threat and is feared in a masculine-oriented society because it stands for "the presence of an otherness that cannot be controlled or manipulated. The world of the feminine seems dark and mysterious, for instance, as in the darkness of the womb which is so closely associated with the unconscious." John Welch distinguishes between the masculine and feminine energies within: "The *anima* is described as that which sees relationships, makes whole, values and reaches out… the anima represents a diffused awareness…." Its opposite is the *animus*, which is described as "the ability to discriminate, focus, differentiate and define… the light of consciousness" (Welch, p. 166). For example, it gives energy to establish and accomplish goals. Not only does the deep feminine help one explore the unconscious, but it also influences his or her way of being.

Ann Belford Ulanov in *Receiving Woman* (pp. 72–73, 77–78) explains why elements of being are associated with the feminine. Our first experience of being is with our mothers. It is there that the specifics of one's *anima* begins to be formed. Almita summarizes Belford's insight: "We are born of woman, we partake of female flesh; we emerge from female bodies which produce food to nourish us. Our mothers are the first to bond with us psychologically. To be flesh of another's flesh—a phrase the Bible uses to connote the deepest intimacies of love—affects who we are and what we become at levels far below consciousness. This feminine element of being has to do with more than our birth for it affects our being alive, being a person, rather than just passively existing. The female element of being links us solidly with our experience of being a distinct 'I,' one bodily and emotionally present, one awaited, recognized, and greeted, one with a capacity to see others as distinctly there, and persons themselves in their own right.

"Associated with the feminine in all of us is the sense of being-at-the-core-of oneself. This involves a capacity to be, to be there calmly, at rest, sensing one's 'self' as somehow found, given, and reflected, instead of achieved, created or manufactured. Being-at-the-core means being vulnerable, as in the intimate mother-child relationship…. We discover this essential 'I am' experience through our dependence on another person seeing and reflecting back to us the fact that 'we are.' The foundation of our capacity **to be** lives in the initial mother-child relationship, though it is not limited to that. That relationship gives us our first taste of being-at-the-core in any significant experience."

Almita goes on to say, "This being-at-the-core is a deep experience of 'I am' and is to be found at the heart of religious experience… the mystery of our being is reflected back to us in the figure of Jesus Christ. He reaches across our broken-apart-being in our counterfeit lives to reestablish us at the core where we find God's being with us." Central to the *Nine Meditations* is the dynamic of Jesus reaching into the directees' wounded areas to bring healing and wholeness in their core. "Therefore, in coming to recognize the deep feminine aspects symbolized by the Samaritan woman, directees can reflect on the deep feminine within themselves as Jesus leads them to experience their own 'I am' in a new and transforming way."

Working against this affirmation of one's being is shame or an inferiority complex. It is the tendency of those who grow up in alcoholic families, those abandoned by parents, or those living in a patriarchal society. Like many women today, the Samaritan woman manifests her low self-esteem by the way she describes herself. She is a Samaritan and a woman, as if these were the worst things anyone could possibly be. This cultural stigma as well as the social stigma of her lifestyle (v. 16–18) probably crushes her spirit. Almita notes, "She would not even dare to show herself or mingle with the other women who came daily to this well in the morning when the weather is cool. Yet none of this is an obstacle to a relationship with Jesus. He desires to have her know him and his love for her removes all barriers. Jesus is able to penetrate through her false image of herself to a place within her that is as yet undiscovered by her. It is the seat of her deepest identity, namely, that she is a child of God, loved and accepted just as she is. This is who Jesus sees. And he believes that if she experiences the depth and breadth of his acceptance and love for her that the inner conversion and transformation will come about in time, as surely as day follows night."

Almita comments on the role of mediation: "From the viewpoint of our Judeo-Christian tradition, the soul has always been represented as female. The soul's flights, mysteries, [and] its patient flowering have ever been linked to a woman's nature. As a result, the woman is endowed with the symbolic burden of being a link, a mediator to another world. The Samaritan woman becomes just such a link and mediator between her people and Jesus who later declares that he does not 'belong to the world' (John 17:14, 16). It is not disputed that the Samaritan woman has a real missionary function, which is made clear by the dialogue between Jesus and his male disciples (vv. 27–38). In this story the woman sows the seed and therefore prepares for apostolic harvest.

"The words the Samaritan woman carries back to her people holds the authority and power of one whose life had been touched and transformed by Jesus. To identify with the Samaritan woman in her missionary role, to see how she… is empowered by Jesus to be a leader and evangelizer, is to deeply listen to the way she now echoes Jesus, for she becomes his voice inviting others, as when he invited the first disciples, to 'Come and see' " (v. 29; see also John 1:39). Men and women who echo this invitation of Jesus to others have to decide first what they want others to experience about Jesus. The Samaritan woman wants others to come and see someone who told her everything she ever did (v. 29). Although initially the townspeople come to hear Jesus because of what the Samaritan woman says, they ultimately believe because they experience Jesus for themselves (v. 42). No human witness can compare with a direct encounter with Jesus."

For women making the retreat there are particular implications. Even though many advances have been made in claiming their equality, dignity, authority and rights (at least in the United States), far too many are still limited like the Samaritan woman. Because she is a "sinner", a Samaritan, and a woman, everything was settled, closed, and defined. There was no hope that her life could be anything different. Almita comments, "Jesus came to crush those lies and banish the evil wrought by self-righteousness, abuse of power and oppression…. Far too many women are still imprisoned by the stereotype images that are projected onto them and by the deep-seated belief that they are somehow inferior by virtue of their sex. Furthermore, the myriad of personal issues or life circumstances that inflict shame and pain can further reinforce their living out of a false sense of who they are."

Almita notes that men also suffer from this same isolation: "Like the Samaritan woman before she met Jesus, men may also have no one to bring them into the light of God's truth. They may have no one to point out options and help them make better choices, no one to tell them about the 'living water' that quenches the deepest human longings, no one to give testimony to the freedom Jesus came to give each and every one." In addition, there is no one to call forth the "deep feminine" within that is so necessary for their wholeness.

She concludes, "The Samaritan woman in this story can be seen as a symbol of all that remains hidden or untapped in us, of all that keeps us from achieving our unique potential, arriving at wholeness and true inner freedom. She represents this *before* her dialogue with Jesus. However, as a result of her dialogue with Jesus the Samaritan woman begins to release the 'deep feminine' within herself. In essence, the deep feminine is the right to *be* and to live out our deepest identity."

Union of Opposites (Thesis, pp. 62–70)

Ultimately, the psyche strives towards wholeness and a balancing of opposites. This process is called *individu-ation*. Almita explains the individuation process further in her thesis: "Individuation is the core process in analytical psychology. It is the goal of life and the way one becomes truly oneself—the person one was intended to be. Individuation, being both a process and a goal, has to do with becoming separate and individual. This separateness means especially separating ourselves from inner compulsions and voices that operate uncon-sciously. As a natural human process and a lifetime goal, individuation is a 'movement toward' rather than ever becoming a finished product. It is an invitation to the journey toward maturity, wholeness, differentiation and integration."

Role of Story and Images (Welch, pp. 26–28, Thesis, pp. 65–66)

This process of individuation is facilitated by the telling of one's story and finding images there to describe who the person is becoming as a result of that narrative. Central to Jung's psychology is the *image* in human experience. Welch observes, "Transforming images which invite conversion abruptly halt my story. The images which arise in the new situation become elements of a new story. By allowing these images to speak to me the narrative of my life story begins again.... In the telling of my experiences through images and words related to those experiences, I begin to own my experiences and allow them to shape me.... In other words, religious experience is not religious experience until it is communicated.... I communicate it when I find some way of paying attention to and reflecting upon the experience."

In referring to the dynamics in the story of the disciples on the way to Emmaus (Luke 24:13–35), he com-ments: "... storying happens not only through the recounting of events but through careful attention to non-reflective, spontaneous imagery that communicates depth experiences. This imagery, rooted in a level below conscious grasp, helps to turn the events of the days into meaningful invitations to enter life more fully and recognize the Lord." Thus, the storying through journal reflection and communication between the director and the directee within the Samaritan Woman Directed Retreat enables individuation.

In her thesis, Almita concludes, "Individuation demands a complete turnabout and is therefore a process of spiritual conversion. Whereas in the first half of life we struggle to build a strong identity and ego in order to deal with, live in, and adapt to the outer world, we are now called to relativize our ego and allow the *Self*... to become the central force of our lives." While the spiritual journey that leads to union with God is not the same as the individuation process, they are related. "The God of grace who draws an individual to seek and find God is the author of all natural processes and therefore of the individuation process as well."

Mandalas as a Symbol of Individuation (Welch, pp. 30–36)

St. Teresa of Avila communicated her story of growing in union with God using the metaphor of a journey to the center of a castle in her classic work, *The Interior Castle*. A brilliant and in-depth exploration of her images in relationship to the individuation process found in Jungian psychology appears in John Welch, O.Carm., *Spiritual Pilgrims: Carl Jung and Teresa of Avila*. One element of Jung's exploration of wholeness discussed there is the tendency of the human psyche to use the sphere or circle to represent its orientation to wholeness or fullness; this image of the psyche Jung called a mandala. Referring to it as "magic circle" and the "nuclear atom of the human psyche," Jung proposed in 1964 that a mandala gives concrete expression not only to the unconscious but also to an evolving Self and consciousness.

The word *mandala* comes from Sanskrit and means "circle." Judith Cornell in her book, *Mandala: Luminous Symbols for Healing*, states that a mandala "is a concrete symbol of its creator's absorption into a sacred center. In its most elevated form, the sacred circle mirrors an illumined state of consciousness through a symbolic pattern—making the invisible visible.... When a practitioner willfully illumines and embodies a sacred image from within the psyche while in a meditative state, spiritual transformation, physical healing, and the integra-tion of personality fragments can result" (Cornell, pp. 2–3). Concentrating on the center of a mandala connects us with both the eternal potential within and the source of the universe. With mystical insight one can grasp the interdependence of all things and all things as one. Many ancient societies have utilized the drawing of a mandala as a prayer and a vehicle for personal transformation.

Teresa's circular castle with God at the center is a mandala. The well and the fountain in the Samaritan woman story are examples of a mandala. Not only is the mandala an expression of the psyche's goal but also it indicates that it has an innate dynamism to move toward its object. "In cases of conflict the psyche often spontaneously produces a mandala as an indication of the possibility of a resolution" (Welch, p. 30). Within the retreat, the directee may be attracted to drawing mandalas. The director may also help a directee notice circular images as they appear in dreams.

"The mandala focuses attention on the center. The circle allows a center to emerge and the center then organizes the chaos about it. Patterns of meaning develop in relationship to the center" (Welch, p. 35). During the course of the Samaritan Woman Directed Retreat the organizing principle seems to shift. Directees begin at the well. They are located at its center and depend upon it for survival. Something in the directees' inner life has caused a thirst deeper and more consuming than a mere physical thirst. By the end of the story, they have replaced the well with the fountain of "living waters," which has as its source and center the Spirit of Jesus. This access to the Spirit re-orients their entire life. They drink now from the presence and the energies that bubble up from within.

Stages (Thesis, pp. 66–67)

Almita looks to Morton Kelsey to identify the stages of individuation. "Morton Kelsey specifies three stages in the pursuit of individuation. The first state is confession—finding out what we are really like in order to transform what needs changing." Utilizing material from the unconscious, this process includes recognizing the shadow. "Transformation is the second stage. This is the capacity to become so close to others that the divine can be manifested in and through the relationship. The final stage is integration—growing more steadfast in our insight and its actualization." In the end, individuation is a mysterious process that guides persons toward their fullest potential.

The psychological process that we know today as individuation seems to be achieved by the Samaritan woman through the guidance of Jesus. She admits her "thirst" (v. 11) and confesses to Jesus (v. 17) that the man she lives with is not her husband; her willingness to dialogue with Jesus opens her to his revelation including his divine identity as Messiah (transformation). Almita writes, "The final stage of integration would have been worked out as the Samaritan woman, now transformed and empowered through her encounter with Jesus, went forth to resolve those 'inner compulsions and voices' that until now controlled her in an unconscious way." Even though the scripture does not tell how this integration was expressed in her life, we do have a sign of this third stage in verses 28–30 in which she becomes a missionary to her people.

Almita continues, "Morton Kelsey goes on to say that integration is learned through practice and experience. The only way a person can come to know his or her soul is to engage in the challenges of inner work. These challenges are what surely faced the Samaritan woman as she returned to the realities of her life situation. True to Jung's theory of individuation, the Samaritan woman went on to actualize her own 'innate capacities to the fullest possible extent and to live out her own individual truth.' For through Jesus, the Creator was guiding her towards her fulfillment." In religious language, individuation is the fulfillment of God's will.

Spiritual Marriage as a Symbol of Individuation (Welch, pp. 165–189)

Especially important in this third stage of individuation is reconciling and embracing the energies of the opposing archetypes—*anima* and *animus*. This process may appear in dream images of marriage or sexual union. In *The Interior Castle*, St. Teresa of Avila uses the image of betrothal and spiritual marriage to express the inexpressible experience of union with God. Welch believes that there is a correlation between this mystical experience and individuation: "Time and time again the human psyche has expressed its rootedness in the ultimate source of meaning through the symbol of marriage. The union of the polarity of the masculine and feminine in marriage has uniquely expressed the deepest unions, the most radical healings experienced by the psyche, the return to the center and source of meaning. Consequently, the marriage symbol, precisely because it is a symbol having layers of references, refers not only to the wedding of the human and divine but also to the integration of the conscious and unconscious poles of personality" (Welch, p. 183). As mentioned in Chapter 8 wells were the meeting place of men and women who would eventually marry. The meeting of Jesus with the Samaritan woman symbolically indicates a future psychic and mystical "marriage." In revealing himself and revealing to her the depths of herself (v. 29), an intimacy, integration and relationship takes place.

Welch continues, "In Jung's theory, the *anima* and *animus*, as inner personalities, mediate the depths of the unconscious to the individual. Just as the persona assists the individual consciousness in relationship to society, so the *anima* and *animus* assist that person in relating to the unknown world of the unconscious. The deeper down the psyche we venture, the more unlike our conscious personalities we find themselves. The shadow is definitely unlike the conscious personality and it resides chiefly in the personal unconscious. But deeper than that, in the collective unconscious, we are so unlike our conscious personality that we even meet a contrasexual side of the psyche, the *anima* or *animus*. To contact one's contrasexual side is to have a doorway to the depths…. If not met and related to, it will act negatively in the unconscious." (Welch, pp. 167–168) Since we develop an awareness of the opposite within us through interaction with the opposite sex, men on this retreat may discover their *anima* as they respond to the Samaritan woman (or a female spiritual director), and women may gain clarity around their *animus* as they encounter Jesus (or a male spiritual director). Jesus, however, as a man in touch with his transformative *anima*, calls both to relationship, risk, and growth.

Directees will find in the journal questions as well as in the symbols of the story an opportunity to meet and embrace their contrasexual side. Answers to questions related to the well and the exploration of one's images and feelings emerge from the unconscious. Being attentive to night dreams, a sense of mission, and the still voice within draws upon the energies of the *anima*. Those allowing for stream of consciousness and active imagination in their writing also rely on the *anima*. On the other hand, these activities call upon the energies of the *animus*: organizing one's life to allow the quiet and focused attention on this retreat; studying the materials; analyzing one's life journey and answering questions related to future changes; and developing a closing ritual. Some parts of this retreat will come more easily, depending on which side of the personality is more developed.

Emergence of the Self (Thesis, pp. 62–70)

Summarizing several sources, Almita writes, "Individuation means becoming one's Self. This movement toward wholeness is the particular adventure of the second half of life… the Self encompasses all the undeveloped potentials, all the unlived life, so now it is much more a life that flows from within, rather than a continuing adaptation to the outside world. In other words when individuals become wedded with the Self, they are no longer being named by their outer environment, people, events, and institutions. It is now their inner environment—their own true Self—that graces them with full acceptance. When taken, this step is a miracle, a conversion, and a new birth. This does not mean that they now negate the outer environment, but rather their orientation is turned around. The 'I' that they had become in the first half of life is no longer in command. The Self that they are called to be, their uniqueness, slowly emerges and gradually takes command. All the unconscious depths within, including repressed memories, are to be discovered and to transform the naming of themselves. This new birth is rightly called the 'change of life' for it is a genuine movement of awesome and earth shaking change. It is an experience of self-affirmation that changes their lives in a way their lives needed to be changed in order to become who they are intended to be.

"The Self is the most important Jungian archetype assuming nearly Godlike proportions. It governs the whole process of individuation, gradually displacing the ego as the center of consciousness. The Self is the sum total of the personality that achieves wholeness."

Applying this individuation process to the Gospel, Almita notes, "The far-reaching effect of the Samaritan woman's dialogue with Jesus is her coming to conversion and rebirth in God. She comes ultimately to live from this newly discovered center, 'God within her.' This dispels the command her pre-individuated state holds over her—the state of being completely and unconsciously identified with an inferior personality. Once she embraces the reality and strength of her most authentic self and once she commits her life to the way of Jesus' teaching, she could begin to move away from those tendencies that contaminate her life." She is free to move toward a life lived out of power and giftedness. Likewise, this individuation process is also possible for the directee through the medium of the *Nine Meditations*.

Spiritual Directors as Midwives of Spiritual Birth

Kelsey affirms the connection between spirituality and psychology: "According to Jung, we cannot grow psychologically unless we grow religiously and we cannot attain our spiritual maturity unless we mature psychologically. He makes the supernatural natural, which makes it even more wonderful. Basically, Jung is saying that we can keep all of our mental capacities and still be effectively religious and transformed by the living God. Although he did not see his function as prescribing a specific religious way, Jung's task was that of a midwife, to bring people to spiritual birth" (Kelsey, pp. 7–8).

Almita concludes then that "spiritual directors are also called to be midwives. And like good midwives, directors bring to their ministry as much knowledge, experience, and expertise as possible from the many sources that can inform them. Jungian psychology is one such rich indispensable source" (Thesis, p. 70).

References

- Bey-Carrión, Almita, *The Samaritan Woman Directed Retreat*
- Brennan, Anne, and Brewi, Janice, *Mid-life Directions: Praying and Playing Sources of New Dynamism*
- Bryant, Christopher, *Jung and the Christian Way*
- Cornell, Judith, *Mandala: Luminous Symbols for Healing*
- Jung, Carl, *Collected Works* Kelsey,
- Morton T., *Christo-Psychology*
- Neumann, Eric, *The Great Mother*
- Ulanov, Ann Belford, *Receiving Woman: Studies in the Psychology and Theology of the Feminine*
- Wehr, Deamris, *Jung and Feminism*
- Welch, John, O.Carm., *Spiritual Pilgrims: Carl Jung and Teresa of Avila*
- Wolff, Hanna, *Jesus the Therapist*
- Yungblut, John R., *The Gentle Art of Spiritual Guidance*

Part IV

Resources

10

The Story Continues

The woman then left her water jar and went off into the town. She said to the people:

"Come and see someone who told me everything I ever did!
Could this not be the Messiah?"

At that they set out from the town to meet him.

Many Samaritans from that town believed in him on the strength of the woman's testimony: "He told me everything I ever did." The result was that, when these Samaritans came to him, they begged him to stay with them awhile. So he stayed there two days, and through his own spoken word many more came to faith. As they told the woman:

"No longer does our faith depend on your story. We have heard for ourselves, and we know that this really is the Savior of the world."

John 4:28–30, 39–42

Testimony from the Reviewers of the Handbook

"Sr. Judy Rinek, S.N.J.M., brings a wealth of experience to those planning to direct individuals in the Woman at the Well retreat. She herself has directed over 30 retreats over the past ten years. In her manual, Conversation and Conversion by the Well, Sr. Judy has collaborated with Almita Bey-Carrión and other seasoned spiritual directors. Based on the narrative of the Samaritan woman at the well from John's Gospel, the retreat integrates sound biblical exegesis along with the Benedictine *Lectio Divina* tradition, and the Ignatian and Twelve Step spirituality. Sr. Judy has provided material, not only for the director, but also for the person making this retreat. Resources, meditations, prayer and bibliography are included in this manual to provide everything necessary for a successful encounter with Jesus who meets each person seeking spiritual growth in their lives."

Kay Murdy, M.A., Co-coordinator of the Catholic Bible Institute sponsored by the Los Angeles Archdiocese and Loyola Marymount University. She is columnist for Ministry and Liturgy Magazine and has authored four books on scripture. The most recent is <u>What Every Catholic Needs to Know about the Bible</u>, published by Resource Publications, Inc.

"I was in transition in my life, taking on new challenges and ways of being, when I began the Samaritan Woman Directed Retreat. The structure of the retreat, and the focus on one scripture passage over several months helped me reflect deeply during that time, and be open to Jesus meeting me in the transition. I always found the meditations perfectly timed and insightful for the next step. Jesus wanted to meet me at my well and break the prison walls that hold me back from the full life of the Spirit in me. For me, that very familiar well will never be the same again! It is truly an inspired retreat, and a gift to walk through it with a retreat director. I know I will be growing into the challenges and discoveries made during this retreat for a long time."

Linda Flynn, Lay Pastoral Counselor and Spiritual Director at La Cañada Presbyterian Church

"... a job well done. Amassing all that data and information must have been a daunting task. To present it in a clear and concise way was a painstaking process."

Fr. Alfred Pooler, C.P., M.A. and D.Min., Spiritual Director and Passionist Preaching Team Member at Mater Dolorosa Passionist Retreat Center

"I felt very inspired and renewed just reading it. I felt as if I had actually been on retreat with you. This book is of great value.... From the healing depths of scripture, Sr. Judy Rinek has brought forth a book of powerful, practical retreat guidance. Focusing on the story in John's Gospel of the encounter between Jesus and the Samaritan woman at the well, Sr. Judy leads us step by step through a meditative retreat of deep healing and spiritual unfoldment. Leaders and participants of such a retreat will experience healing waters flowing from both the reading and the experience."

Flora Slosson Wuellner, M.Div., Author, Retreat Leader and Minister in United Church of Christ

"Congratulations on such an ambitious job! I think that the users of this handbook will be very well prepared to give the retreat, after they have made it themselves... I think this manual would be a great tool for a spiritual director giving any kind of retreat, not just this one!

Sr. Barbara Williams, S.N.J.M., Ph.D., Spiritual Director with a specialty in the Nineteen Annotation of the Spiritual Exercises of St. Ignatius

"You have done a really fine job! This manual is a wonderful contribution to those who direct the Samaritan Woman Directed Retreat. To have all this information gathered together in one place is a great help to those giving this retreat."

Sr. Carol Ries, S.N.J.M., M.S. and M.S.W., Spiritual Director and Certified Consultant of Mid-Life and Long-Life Directions

"The amount and quality of information you have gathered in this handbook is remarkable. It reflects months of careful and dedicated work, and should be a great help to those who will use it."

Sr. Thomas Bernard, C.S.J., M.A., Spiritual Director and Director of Spiritual Growth Center in Los Angeles, California, a training center for spiritual directors.

11

Appendix: What Additional Resources Are Suggested for this Retreat?

Refer to Chapter 4, "Enhancements to the Meditations," for guidelines in using these and other resources for the retreat. You may want to retype the handouts and embellish them with graphics or borders to make them more attractive. Letters and surveys are templates to help you create your own. If you use the prayers and quotations written by other authors, please acknowledge them. In the bibliography are many insightful books in which to glean other prayers and resources.

At the end of this section you will find a list of spiritual directors who give this retreat with their contact information, and a feedback form to assist in the on-going development of this handbook. The spiritual directors who helped put this handbook together hope that this information has given enough depth in understanding the nature of the retreat, provided very practical ways to facilitate the retreat, and encouraged you to follow the Spirit with confidence as you participate in this sacred and powerful ministry.

Sequence of Resources:

Before the retreat:

- "What is Spiritual Direction?" compiled by Sandra Linderman
- Sample cover letter for potential directee and survey
- Your life is a sacred journey…" by Carolyn Joy Adams

First Meditation:

- Meditation on the shrine of Jacob's Well by Almita Bey-Carriòn
- "The Journey" by Mary Oliver
- Psalm 139 by Emily Nabholz, S.C.N.
- "Our deepest fear…" by Marianne Williamson
- Mohini, the Tiger as told by Charles "Tom" Brown

Second Meditation:

- "Imagine a Woman" by Patricia Lynn Reilly
- "Loosen My Grip" by Ted Loder
- "The Shadow" summarized from Catholic Women Network

Third Meditation:

- "Above all, trust…" by Pierre de Chardin, S.J.
- "Into the hands…" by Pierre de Chardin, S.J.
- "If You Only Knew" by Adrian Van Kaam, C.S.Sp
- "Inner Freedom" by Joyce Rupp, O.S.M.

Fourth Meditation:

- Story: "The Cracked Pot"

Fifth Meditation:

- "But I believe…" by Rainer Maria Rilke
- "Only still waters…" by Raymond B. Walker and "God, grant me the serenity…" by Reinhold Neibuhr
- "Let Your God Love You"

Sixth Meditation:

- "My Lord God, I have no idea…" by Thomas Merton and "There is a pearl…" by Gregory Norbet
- "This is Jesus to me…" by Mother Theresa of Calcutta
- "The Deer's Cry" attributed to St. Patrick

Seventh Meditation:

- "Wordless Praise to Sophia" by Joyce Rupp, O.S.M.
- "Empowered Vulnerability" guided meditation by Flora Slosson Wuellner
- "Ours is not the task…" by Clarissa Pinkola-Estes

Eighth Meditation:

- Prayer: "The Blessing Cup" by Joyce Rupp, O.S.M.
- "It helps, now and then…" Archbishop Oscar Romero
- "Christ in my mind…" by Janet Morley

Ninth Meditation:

- Examen

Other Resources:

- Present Spiritual Directors for the Samaritan Woman Directed Retreat
- Response to Handbook Survey

What is Spiritual Direction?

Compiled by Sandra Linderman

Life is a sacred journey. During our journey we can experience times of great spiritual growth, challenges, or yearnings. We may even experience "desert" times—that is, times of dryness, doubt and darkness. To have a trained person to be a companion and guide during our spiritual journey is what spiritual direction is all about.

Spiritual direction can be a misleading term because it is NOT telling another person what to do or telling them what God is doing in their lives. Spiritual friend or spiritual companion better describes what takes place in a relationship with a spiritual director. In spiritual direction we look at our lives and realize that even in mundane and everyday events God is trying to reach us. The director, in a listening role, helps us to be open to the inner nudging of the Spirit. We are called into a deeper relationship with God by one who offers us a safe place for exploring Mystery, by one who asks questions for clarification, observes and suggests. Above all, the director helps us pay attention to our religious experience—notice it, embrace it, and allow it to transform our mind, body, and spirit. A director does not need to be wiser, holier or have had exactly the same experience as the directee to be a helpful companion. The Holy Spirit is the true director and both have to be open and to be listening for the voice of the Spirit.

This ministry goes back before the Fourth Century when people sought out the desert Fathers and Mothers for spiritual guidance. It became more popular with the growth of the monastic communities and the influence of religious mystics, such as Julian of Norwich, St. John of the Cross, St. Teresa of Avila and Hildegard of Bingen. Throughout the ages as people became more aware of God's call to a deep personal relationship, they sought out the prayerful discernment of others—religious or lay.

For our own time, this ministry is becoming very popular and relevant. Since we tend to be very busy, we may have distanced ourselves from God. As we share everyday events, questions, doubts, sorrows, and joys, the director helps us focus on what God is saying to us in the midst of the craziness of our lives.

February 16, 2005

Dear Darlene,

Thank you for your interest in the Samaritan Woman Directed Retreat. Enclosed are some materials that will give you further background and information, including a survey to return to me. One of the spiritual directors will interview you in the future to assess whether this retreat is right for you and what is the best way to begin; you will also be interviewing her to decide if she would be a good director for you. Since there has been such an interest in this retreat, our present spiritual directors are taking as many people as they can handle through the retreat at this time. Thank you for waiting for the next available opening.

This retreat is especially effective when you are in a transition in your life—graduation, move, change of career, recovery from addiction, conclusion of a relationship, inner shift, new phase of spiritual growth, mid-life crisis, recovery from serious illness and the like. Many times we rely on something in our life which ultimately does not satisfy the deepest longings of our soul. We find ourselves searching but not sure what for or where to find it. This retreat helps you move beyond that reality. It introduces you to a way of praying through writing in your journal and meditating on Chapter 4 of John's Gospel. If you are artistically inclined, you may find drawing, clay, music, dance, dreams, ritual, etc. especially expressive of your inner life. Time in individual spiritual direction includes the reading of what you have written, questions for clarification, and exploration of what God is saying to you, personally, through this very powerful story. It is one to be truly savored! **Did you know that the Samaritan woman's story is your story, also?** It has been very transforming for those who have made this journey.

Part of your commitment is taking enough time for honest reflection to complete the journal questions provided for each session. The individual spiritual direction lasts 1 ½ to 2 hours. You would pay for each session, one session at a time (the spiritual director will let you know the amount). At any time you may decide not to continue.

Before you have your first official session of the retreat, please write out (or draw) the highlights of your spiritual journey—major challenges and breakthroughs, how God has been present to you and you to God, and why you seek this retreat at this time in your life. Please, return the survey in the envelope provided to me as soon as possible; your director will call you to confirm arrangements. Especially if you have not experienced regular spiritual direction or Scriptural meditation, she may ask to meet with you for several times before the retreat begins.

Peace in Christ,

Sr. Judy Rinek, S.N.J.M.
Mater Dolorosa Retreat Center

Survey of Interest for Samaritan Women Retreat

Send to: Sr. Judy Rinek, SNJM
                    Mater Dolorosa Passionist Retreat Center
                    700 N. Sunnyside Ave.
                    Sierra Madre, CA 91024

Name _____

Mailing
Address _____

_____

Home Phone ( ) _____ Work Phone ( ) _____

E-Mail
Address: _____

Past experience with spiritual direction? ____ yes ____ no   Therapy? ____ yes ____ no

Present religion/denomination _____

Specify other growth experiences (workshops, retreats, travel, studies, etc.)

Earliest month/year that you can begin this retreat: _____

Are you available for a 1 ½ to 2 hour session in   _____ daytime? _____ eves? _____

                                      best time(s) _____

Preference for sessions: daily   (10 days) ____ weekly (10 weeks) _____

                                      every 2 weeks (20 weeks) _____

Type of spiritual director desired for this retreat—e.g., background, religious tradition

Why seeking this retreat/specialized spiritual direction at this time?

Your life is a
sacred journey

*And it is about change, growth, discovery,
movement, transformation, continuously
expanding your vision of what is possible,
stretching your soul, learning to see clearly &
deeply, listening to your intuition, taking
courageous risks, embracing challenges at every
step along the way…*

You are on the path

*Exactly where you are meant to be right now…
And from here, you can only go forward,
shaping your life story into a magnificent tale
of triumph, of healing, of courage, beauty,
wisdom, power, dignity & love…*

Carolyn Joy Adams

Shrine at Jacob's Well

As you meditate on this picture, what do you notice? What does this photo tell you about your well? What follows is a reflection of Almita Bey-Carrión on a photograph of a Greek Orthodox Church that enshrines Jacob's Well in the town of Nablus.

What strikes me is how much rope is needed to lower the bucket. Our wells go deep. Also, looking at the well I realize that the water being drawn is in the bowels of the earth... in the darkness. So, too, our "well" as we come to know it through the retreat, is in the bowels of our personal darkness or shadow side. Like the Samaritan woman, we come *alone* to draw this "water" that quenches our thirst temporarily. We don't want anyone to see us or be aware of our dysfunction (unless, of course our "well" should involve another person or people, as in sexual or substance abuse addictions). Then Jesus shows up...

Another thought that comes to me is that this well is made by human beings. Our wells are also made by us, usually in response to an experience or circumstances that resulted in our feeling a need to "construct" a well we could return to again and again, trying to quench a thirst or a need. Jesus comes to offer water, not from a self-constructed well, but spiritual water from heaven that will never run dry.

The Journey

One day you finally knew
what you had to do, and began,
though the voices around you
kept shouting
their bad advice—
though the whole house
began to tremble
and you felt the old tug
at your ankles.
"Mend my life!"
each voice cried.
But you didn't stop.
You knew what you had to do,
though the wind pried
with its stiff fingers
at the very foundations—
though their melancholy
was terrible.
It was already late
enough, and a wild night,
and the road full of fallen
branches and stones.
But little by little,
As you left their voices behind,
the stars began to burn
through the sheets of clouds,
and there was a new voice,
which you slowly
recognized as your own
that kept you company
as you strode deeper and deeper
into the world,
determined to do
the only thing you could do—
determined to save
the only life you could save.

By Mary Oliver from **Dream Work**

Psalm 139 A Woman's Psalm

You have searchd me and know me

I am woman… on a journey through life
I am searching my innermost self to claim who I am as woman
I am searching for you, my God
I am going beyond reflections…

I am woman on an inner search

This inner search leads me to stop running away from you
… to trust in ever abiding presence
… to trust your inner working in me as woman

I am woman full of light and shadows
                    full of love and fear
                    full of hope and despair

But your are there to lead me… to help me
You are the light of my life
I could ask the darkness to hide me
You call me out of darkness
Darkness and light are the same to you
You accept me just as I am

A woman of light and shadows
                love and fear
                hope and despair

You accept me and call me to a deep inner life of presence
and relationship… even when I am alone and encompassed by me
and my shadow.

As I look around and remember your goodness to me
My heart is glad
As woman, I ever seek you in all your ways.

You created every part of me
You put me together in my mother's womb,
In the womb of life, I am nurtured and nourished, protected and loved,
I praise you for the gift of life… for the gift of being woman.

I am woman remembering the child in me.
I am the Wind, the Earth, the Fire, and the Water of Life
When I was a child I thought and spoke, trusted and loved as a child.
You played with me, ran with me, protected me.
You called me to be a child of God… you were there beside me.

And now that I am grown, I am a woman. You continue to call me
To come forth from my tombs of fear and isolation into who I am as a woman.
I feel a sense of discovery, of having touched Life and being called
To go deeper and beyond into KNOWING and LOVING.
You fill me with your presence as I empty myself, standing still, waiting…

I am a woman of consolation and desolation
I am a mother, a sister, a woman of sorrow, a woman maturing
A woman walking along side of you—a man of sorrows who brings LIFE
out of pain, suffering, sorrow, losses and death.

As a woman, I walk too, with you, along side of and in support of
my brothers and sisters who struggle with life and death –
The fine line, the tight rope between life and death.

I am woman in touch with all aspects of my growing, evolving,
Becoming who you called me—unique, special, precious.
My search for wholeness and holiness comes to rest in your presence,
I let go of my life and let integration take place, and I am "at home."
As I continue to grow, new life comes from embracing my whole life process:

      all the lights and the shadows
      all the pain and joy
      all hopes and disappointments.

Examine me, O Lord, and know me through and through.
Let me be naked and open before you, for you are my God.
I am woman in awe and praise of you.
Teach me to pray.
Pray within me, my Lord and my God.

Emily Nabholz, S.C.N.

Our deepest fear is not that we are inadequate.
Our deepest fear is that we are powerful
beyond measure.
It is our light, not our darkness,
that most frightens us.
We ask ourselves, who am I to be brilliant,
gorgeous, talented and fabulous?
Actually, who are you NOT to be?
You are a child of God.
Your playing small doesn't serve the world.
There's nothing enlightened about shrinking
so that other people won't feel
insecure around you.
We are born to make manifest
the glory of God that is within us.
It is not just in some of us: it's in everyone.
And as we let our own light shine,
we unconsciously
give other people permission to do the same.
As we are liberated from our own fear,
our presence automatically
liberates others.

Marianne Williamson from **A Return to Love**

Mohini, the Tiger

This story is reflected upon by inmate Charles "Tom" Brown from prison in Buckeye, Arizona.

Mohini, a white tiger, spent years pacing back and forth in her twelve-by-twelve-foot cage in the National Zoo in Washington, D.C. Eventually, a natural habitat was created for her. Covering several acres, it had hills, trees, a pond, and a variety of vegetation. With excitement and anticipation, the staff released Mohini into her new and expansive environment. The tiger immediately sought refuge in the corner of the compound. There she lived for the remainder of her life, pacing back and forth in an area measuring twelve feet by twelve feet.

Some prisons are built with concrete, steel, and razor wire. Others are built in the dungeons of our minds. Though freedom is possible, we often pass our years trapped in the same old patterns. We cage ourselves in to self-imposed prisons with self-judgment and anxiety. Then, with the passing of time, we like Mohini, grow incapable of accessing the freedom and peace that is our birthright.

Life, however, is continually calling us to be more, to journey into the wilderness and face the truth. In my case, the shell of my life had to be softened—broken down, even—by the experience of coming to prison, before the moment of truth could appear. I needed to be humbled, cooked in tears of loss, for any deeper life to emerge.

A new life requires a death of some kind; otherwise, it is nothing new but the shuffling of the same old deck. What dies is an outworn way of being in the world. We are no longer who we thought we were.

On the deepest level, this journey of awakening opens us up to the innermost center of love. Love creates its own freedom from imprisonment, has its own direction, moves according to its own rhythms, and makes it own music.

Imagine a Woman

Imagine a woman who believes it is right and good she is a woman,
A woman who honors her experience and tells her stories,
Who refuses to carry the sins of others within her body and life.

Imagine a woman who believes she is good,
A woman who trusts and respects herself,
Who listens to her needs and desires
        and then meets them with tenderness and grace.

Imagine a woman who believes she belongs in the world,
A woman who celebrates her own life,
Who is glad to be alive.

Imagine a woman who has acknowledged
        the past's influence on the present.
A woman who has walked through her past,
Who has healed into the present.

Imagine a woman in love with her own body,
A woman who believes her body is enough, just as it is,
Who celebrates her body as a trustworthy companion
        and its rhythms and cycles as an exquisite resource.

Imagine a woman who embraces her sexuality as her own…
Who experiences all of her erotic feelings and sensations
        without shame or guilt.

Imagine a woman who honors the face of the Goddess
        in her own changing face,
A woman who celebrates the accumulation of her years
        and her wisdom.
Who refuses to use her precious life energy to
        disguise the changes in her body and life.

Imagine a woman who authors her own life,
A woman who exerts, initiates, and moves on her own behalf,
Who refuses to surrender except to her truest self
        and to her wisest voice.

Imagine a woman who names her own gods,
A woman who imagines the divine in her own image and likeness,
Who designs her own spirituality
        and allows it to inform her daily life.

Imagine a woman who values the women in her life,
A woman who sits in circles of women,
Who is reminded of the truth about herself when she forgets.
Imagine a shameless woman who is full of herself.
A powerful woman who has awakened to the truth about herself.
A courageous woman who has assumed her rightful place beside men.
A wise woman whose beliefs about herself are reflected
        in her relationships.

Imagine yourself as this woman

as you gather the gifts of your awakening:

A freed imagination, a God born of your own experience as a woman, the unfolding images of your spiritual center; a suspicion of the customary, a courageous rebellion, a commitment to shape your own life and spirituality; the celebration of your body and natural processes, the accumulation of your years, the rich resources of wisdom within you; an affirmation of your goodness, an acknowledgment of your wounds, an experience of healing into the present.

Gather these gifts and offer them to your mothers, daughters, granddaughters and nieces. To your fathers, sons, grandsons, and nephews. Offer them to your lovers and friends. To a world out of balance, estranged from wisdom and addicted to power.

The feminine has been exiled. She groans through our wounded bodies, our severed relationships and broken earth. We call upon her to return and teach us new ways of living and being, new ways of relating to each other. We invite her out of exile as we reclaim our original goodness, power, courage, independence, sensuality, divinity, wholeness, and wisdom. It is through us that she is present in the world.

by Patricia Lynn Reilly from **A God Who Looks Like Me**

Loosen my Grip

O God, it is hard for me to let go,
        most times,
and the squeeze I exert
        garbles me and gnarls others.
So loosen by grip a bit
        on the good times,
                on the moments of sunlight and star shine and joy,
that the thousand graces they scatter as they pass
        may nurture growth in me
                rather than turn to brittle memories.

Loosen my grip
        on those grudges and grievances
                I hold so closely,
that I may risk exposing myself
        to the spirit of forgiving and forgiveness
                that changes things and resurrects dreams and
                        courage.

Loosen my grip
        on my fears
that I may be released a little into humility
        and into an acceptance of my humanity.

Loosen my grip
        on myself
that I may experience the freedom of a fool
        who knows that to believe
                is to see kingdoms, find power, sense glory;
to reach out
        is to know myself held;
to laugh at myself
        is to be the joke of your grace;
        to attend to each moment
                is to hear the faint melody of eternity;
        to dare to love
                is to smell the wild flowers of heaven.

Loosen my grip
        on my ways and words,
                on my fears and fretfulness
that letting go
        into the depths of silence
                and my own uncharted longings,
I may find myself held by you
        and linked anew to all life
                in this wild and wondrous world
                        you love so much,
so that I may take to heart
        that you have taken me to heart.

by Ted Loder from **Guerrillas of Grace**

The Shadow

Summarized from an article in "Catholic Women's Network," Jan/Feb 1995

"We must learn to recognize our shadow side if we are to develop a whole personality and to live by an appropriate moral code." John Sanford

John Sanford believes the function of the ego is to lead us to consciousness but is often lazy. Few people become conscious without having to, so evil is the prod. Pain, loss, and tragedy in life nudge people toward consciousness, toward individuation. This is where the shadow side comes in.

Shadow is a psychological concept which refers to the "dark, feared, unwanted" side of human personality. As we develop, we all try to embody in ourselves a particular image of what we want to be. The qualities we reject constitute our shadow side.

When society or our parents tell us not to murder, steal or lie, we try to conform and reject or repress the thief and murderer in ourselves. Our Christian tradition tells us to be loving, forgiving, and chaste, and in trying to achieve these, we reject the part of ourselves that gets angry, mean, and sexually uncontrolled. However, to accept these parts does not lead to hurtful actions.

These things we reject do not disappear. They live on within us as our Shadow. When we dream, the Shadow always appears as a female figure (male for men) that we dislike or react to in a negative way. It represents qualities we could have developed. 98% of the Shadow is "gold" if we learn to recognize it and engage its energies to provide balance in our life. The process of recognizing and integrating the opposite sides of our personality is called individuation.

By mid-life, many of our energies may be running out and we have to draw on the energies of our unlived lives. If we live lives of constantly giving and serving others, we may repress our own needs. These may be stored as anger or resentment. When our situation becomes intolerable, we may react in anger which energizes us to balance our giving with our own need to receive. Individuals who deny sexuality need to get in contact with their sexuality if they are to become whole. Those who deny anger or greed must confront it in order to integrate it.

Humor is one clue to our shadow. Examine what strikes you as humorous, because it us usually the shadow side that makes us laugh or is released in laughter. If the Shadow is too repressed, people will lack a sense of humor and be judging and unforgiving.

Other clues: **Slips of the tongue—misstatements are often the shadow talking**
Unconscious forgetting—accepting an invitation and then forgetting to show up may be a message from the shadow
Fantasies—of sexual conquest, violence, power or money are expressions of the shadow
Listing of strengths—all the opposites are in your shadow

Caution: **To deny the Shadow completely may cause all life energies to dry up. There are times when the unlived life must surface if we are to gain new energy to live. If we strive to be good and truthful, we may become hateful if too much energy is denied. When we try to exceed our capacity for goodness, we bring about evil because our unnatural stance generates an accumulation of darkness in the unconscious.**

Above all, trust in the slow work of God.
We are, quite naturally impatient in everything
to reach the end without delay.
We should like to skip
the intermediate stages.
We are impatient of being on
the way to something unknown, something new,
and yet it is the law of all progress
that it is made by passing through
some stages of instability—
and that it may take a very long time.
And so I think it is with you.
Your ideas mature gradually—let them grow,
let them shape themselves,
without undue haste.
Don't try to force them on,
as though you could be today
what time (that is to say, grace
and circumstances acting on your own good will)
will make them tomorrow.
Only God could say what this new spirit
gradually forming within you will be.
Give Our Lord the benefit of believing
that his hand is leading you,
and accept the anxiety of
feeling yourself in suspense and incomplete.

Pierre Teilhard de Chardin
from **Letter to Two Friends**

Into the hands which broke
and quickened the bread,
which blessed and caressed little children,
which were pierced with nails,
into the hands which are like our hands –
the hands of which one can never tell what they
will do with the object they are holding –
whether they will break it or heal it,
but which we know will always obey
and reveal impulses filled with kindness
and will always clasp us
ever more closely, ever more jealously:

Into the gentle and mighty hands
which can reach down
into the very depths of the soul,
the hands which fashion,
which create—the hands through
which flows out so great a love:

Into these hands it is comforting
to surrender oneself, especially
if one is suffering or afraid.
And there is both great happiness
and great merit in so doing.

Pierre Teilhard de Chardin

If You Only Knew

If you only knew that I am the incarnation of the
Infinite Love you have been longing for deep in
your heart.

If you only knew that my longing for you
surpasses infinitely your longing for me.

If you only knew that I am burning with desire to
fill you with the living water of grace and love,
that my asking you anything is but a loving
occasion for me to touch you, to make you into a
new person.

If you only knew that I cannot do so without
your being receptive to me, then you would ask me to
give you a drink of divine compassion and I
would give you that living water.

To really reach you, I need your asking. Without
your receptivity I can do nothing. I am powerless
in my love for you.

By Adrian Van Kaam, C.S.Sp from **The Woman at the Well**

Inner Freedom

Liberating Spirit,
part of me has forgotten
the freedom of self-acceptance,
the putting aside of what others think,
the quieting of the inner voices
that demand, nag and whine.

Part of me has stopped believing
in my potential for growth,
in the possibilities of my dreams,
in the grace of my prayer.

Part of me holds too tightly
to what the ego knows,
to securities that have grown stale,
to fears that stand in domination.

I want to remember
my inner wings.
I want to soar free
under the welcoming sky
of personal freedom.

Winged One, Free One,
enter my imprisoned self.
Break the bonds
that clasp my spirit.
Whisper in my soul's ear:
"Wings, wings,
remember your wings!"

by Joyce Rupp, O.S.M. from **Prayers to Sophia**

THE CRACKED POT

A water bearer in India had two large pots, each hung on each end of a pole which he carried across his neck. One of the pots had a crack in it, and while the other pot was perfect and always delivered a full portion of water at the end of the long walk from the stream to the master's house, the cracked pot arrived only half full.

For a full two years this went on daily, with the bearer delivering only one and a half pots full of water in his master's house. Of course, the perfect pot was proud of its accomplishments, perfect to the end for which it was made. But the poor cracked pot was ashamed of its own imperfection and miserable that it was able to accomplish only half of what it had been made to do.

After two years of what it perceived to be a bitter failure, it spoke to the water bearer one day by the stream, "I am ashamed of myself, and I want to apologize to you." "Why?" asked the bearer. "What are you ashamed of?" "I have been able, for these past two years, to deliver only half my load, because this crack in my side causes water to leak out all the way back to your master's house. Because of my flaws, you have to do all of this work, and you don't get full value from your efforts," the pot said.

The water bearer felt sorry for the old cracked pot, and in his compassion he said, "As we return to the master's house, I want you to notice the beautiful flowers along the path." Indeed, as they went up the hill, the old cracked pot took notice of the sun warming the beautiful wild flowers on the side of the path, and this cheered it some. But at the end of the trail, it still felt bad because it had leaked out half its load, and so again it apologized to the bearer for its failure.

The bearer said to the pot, "Did you notice that there were flowers only on your side of your path, but not on the other pot's side? That's because I have always known about your flaw, and I took advantage of it. I planted flower seeds on your side of the path, and every day while we walk back from the stream, you've watered them. For two years I have been able to pick these beautiful flowers to decorate my master's table. Without you being just the way you are, he would not have this beauty to grace his house."

Each of us has our own unique flaws. We are all cracked pots. But if we will allow it, the Lord will use our flaws. In God's great economy, nothing goes to waste. Don't be afraid of your flaws. Acknowledge them, and take advantage of them, and you, too, can be the cause of beauty in your pathway. Go out boldly, knowing that in our weakness we find strength. (Cf. 2 Corinthians 12:7–10)

Anonymous

cf. Willy McNamara from **Chicken Soup for the Unsinkable Soul**

But I believe nevertheless that you will not have
to remain without a solution if you will hold to objects
that are similar to those from which my eyes
now draw refreshment.
If you will cling to Nature, to the simple in Nature,
to the little things that hardly anyone sees,
and that can so unexpectedly become big and beyond measuring;
if you have this love of inconsiderable things
and seek quite simply, as one who serves,
to win the confidence of what seems poor:
then everything will become easier, more coherent
and somehow more conciliatory for you,
not in your intellect, perhaps, which lags marveling behind,
but in your inmost consciousness, waking and cognizance.

You are so young, so before all beginning,
and I want to beg you, as much as I can, dear sir,
to be patient toward all that is unsolved in your heart
and to try to love the questions themselves
like locked rooms and like books that are written
in a very foreign tongue.
Do not now seek the answers, which cannot be given you
because you would not be able to live them.
And the point is to live everything. Live the questions now.
Perhaps you will then gradually, without noticing it,
live along some distant day into the answer.
Perhaps you do carry within yourself
the possibility of shaping and forming
as a particularly happy and pure way of living;
train yourself to it—but take whatever comes with great trust,
and if only it comes out of your own will,
out of some need of your inmost being,
take it upon yourself and hate nothing....

Rainer Maria Rilke
from **Letters to a Young Poet**

Only still waters can reflect nature's splendor.
Serenity is not attained by exertion -
only in quietness of soul is it realized,
for tranquility and peace are reflected virtues.

How shall we learn to be still?

Leave the disturbing moment
where gusts of pain or drifts of weariness ruffle your spirit;
go in memory or imagination to nature's still waters:
some quiet pool where majesty is mirrored.

Turbulence would erase the beauty
and distort the reflection of surrounding loveliness.
Sang the Psalmist: "He leadeth me beside still waters…"
Let the Shepherd of Serenity guide your thoughts, your mood,
and you will attain the calmness that banishes distortion.
All about you are the glories of life:
The beauty and strength of the universe,
The changeless love of God.

Raymond B. Walker
from **Beside Still Waters**

God, grant me the serenity
to accept the things I cannot change,
courage to change the things I can,
and the wisdom to know the difference.

Living one day at a time,
enjoying one moment at a time.
Accepting hardships as the pathway to peace.
Taking, as He did, this sinful world as it is, not as I would have it.
Trusting that He will make all things right if I surrender to His will:
that I may be reasonably happy in this life,
and supremely happy with Him forever.

Reinhold Neibuhr

Let Your God Love You

Be silent.
Be still.
Alone. Empty
Before your God.
Say nothing.
Ask nothing.
Be silent.
Be still.

Let your God
Look upon you.
That is all.
God knows
And understands.
God loves you with
An enormous love,
Wanting only to

Look upon you
With Love.
Quiet.
Still.
Be.

Let your God—
Love you.

Anonymous

My Lord God, I have no idea where I am going.
I do not see the road ahead of me.
I cannot know for certain where it will end.
Nor do I really know myself,
and the fact that I think I am following your will
does not actually mean that I am doing so.

But I believe that the desire to please you does
in fact please you.
And I hope I have that desire in all that I am doing.
I hope that I will never do anything apart from that desire.
And I know that if I do this you will lead me by the right road,
though I may know nothing about it.

Therefore will I trust you always,
though I seem lost and in the shadow of death.
I will not fear, for you are ever with me,
and you will never leave me to face my perils alone.

Thomas Merton

There is a pearl of great price
WITHIN YOU.
It is your hidden self where God abides,
the seed of all goodness and love,
the power of all that is wholesome and lifegiving!
It is your faith,
your inner child of wonder and delight,
of guilessness and enthusiasm.
It is your wellspring of hospitality,
where you are host & hostess for a banquet
of simple sharing and profound transformation.
May you always honor the greatness of your soul
and nurture that place of being
from which others drink deeply.

Gregory Norbet

This is Jesus to me
        The Word made flesh
        The Bread of Life

The Word	to be spoken
The Truth	to be told
The Way	to be walked
The Light	to be spread
The Life	to be lived
The Love	to be loved
The Joy	to be shared
The Sacrifice	to be offered
The Peace	to be given
The Bread of Life	to be eaten
The Hungry	to be fed
The Thirsty	to be satisfied
The Naked	to be clothed
The Homeless	to be taken in
The Lonely	to be loved
The Unwanted	to be wanted
The Leper	to be washed
The Beggar	to be assisted
The Drunkard	to be listened to
The Mentally Ill	to be protected
The Little One	to be embraced
The Blind	to be led
The Dumb	to be spoken for
The Crippled	to be walked with
The Drug Addict	to befriend
The Prostitute	to remove from danger
The Prisoner	to be visited
The Old	to be served

To me,   Jesus is my God
              Jesus is my Spouse
              Jesus is my Life
              Jesus is my only Love
              Jesus is my All in All
              Jesus is my Everything

Mother Theresa of Calcutta

The Deer's Cry (selections) attributed to St. Patrick

I arise today
Through the strength of Heaven

Light of Sun
Radiance of Moon
Splendor of Fire
Speed of Lightning
Swiftness of Wind
Depth of the Sea
Stability of Earth
Firmness of Rock

I arise today
Through God's strength to pilot me
God's eye to look before me
God's wisdom to guide me
God's way to lie before me
God's shield to protect me

From all who wish me ill
Afar and anear, alone and in a multitude
Against every cruel, merciless power
That may oppose my body and soul.

Christ with me
Christ before me
Christ behind me
Christ in me
Christ beneath me
Christ above me
Christ on my right
Christ on my left
Christ when I lie down
Christ when I sit down
Christ when I arise
Christ to shield me

Christ in the heart of everyone who thinks of me
Christ in the mouth of everyone who speaks of me.

I arise today.

Wordless Praise to Sophia

Wise One who claims my heart,
how can I name you to others?
How can I ever capture
the reflection of your radiance
rising in profuse grandeur
on the glittering sea of my soul?
It is like trying to capture
the essence of a harvest moon
rising in full orange orbness,
sparkling glory on a September sea.

Some moments have no words.
Some relationships have no narration.
They rise silently like the swelling path
of the full moon in a harvest sky,
like the soundless rise and fall
on the breath of one who sleeps gently.

No need to capture, control, contain,
only to be present to the rising,
only to be aware of the silent breathing,
only to be with the unexpected illumination.

It is enough to rest in your love.
It is enough to taste your goodness.
It is enough to call you by name.
It is enough. It is enough.

by Joyce Rupp, O.S.M. from **Prayers to Sophia**

Guided Meditation: *"Empowered Vulnerability"*
by Flora Slosson Wuellner from **Release**

> "They are like trees
> planted by streams of water,
> which yield their fruit in its season."
> Psalm 1:3

Make your whole body comfortable in whatever way is best for you, whether sitting up or lying down. Breathe in and out, slowly, gently, fully, without any pushing, from the soles of your feet to the top of your head. Let the breath flow through you like a quiet river of light. Take as long as you need to feel God's peace.

You may choose to stay with the quiet breathing of the light through your body. But if you feel ready, think of a strong, healthy tree, with roots thrust deep in the earth. Picture the wide interlacing of the roots, like veins and arteries, searching out the underground springs of water, absorbing the moisture and the soil's rich nourishment. The taproot goes deepest of all, down to deeper levels of water. Stay focused on the roots as long as you wish, while they drink.

When ready, picture or just sense the nutrients and moisture flowing higher up the tree, slowly, but fully, into the trunk, the branches, the twigs, the leaves. The whole thirsty tree is drinking in all that it needs.

When you feel ready, think of those wide-spreading, stretching branches. They stretch into the air as high as the roots stretch deep into the earth. See the leaves receiving the particles of gold sunlight. Let the golden light flow through each leaf, each twig, down through the branches, the tree trunk, and into the roots. Let every tiny root be filled with the power of the sunlight.

Stay with this image as long as you wish. When ready, sense or picture the sunlight from the leaves and the moisture from the earth mingling together, flowing with quiet power throughout the whole tree.

If there is anything that is not right for the tree, infection, insect invasion, dark spots, let it go out of the tree, down through the tap-root, deep into the ground, down to the very center of the earth. You do not need to know necessarily what that is that is being sent out of the tree. It is enough to know that the tree is being cleansed of what does not belong to it.

Rest yourself in this picture for as long as you wish. Think of yourself as this strong, flexible tree. As you breathe each gentle breath, let the roots go deeper and the branches expand wider. The tree can sway and bend with ease because the roots are so deep and strong. The tree can breathe the world's air because it will be cleansed of what it does not need, what does not belong to it.

When you feel ready to close your meditation, take a few moments of silence as you prepare for re-entry into your everyday life. In the days to come, often look into your heart at your radiant tree of empowered vulnerability.

OURS IS NOT THE TASK of fixing the entire world all at once, but of stretching out to mend the part of the world that is within our reach. Any small, calm thing that one soul can do to help another soul, to assist some portion of this poor suffering world, will help immensely. It is not given to us to know which acts or by whom, will cause the critical mass to tip toward an enduring good. What is needed for dramatic change is an accumulation of acts, adding, adding to, adding more, continuing. We know that it does not take "everyone on Earth" to bring justice and peace, but only a small, determined group who will not give up during the first, second, or hundredth gale.

One of the most calming and powerful actions you can do to intervene in a stormy world is to stand up and show your soul. Soul on deck shines like gold in dark times. The light of the soul throws sparks, can send up flares, builds signal fires, causes proper matter to catch fire. To display the lantern of soul in shadowy times like these--to be fierce and to show mercy toward others, both are acts of immense bravery and greatest necessity. Struggling souls catch light from other souls who are fully lit and willing to show it. If you would help to calm the tumult, this is one of the strongest things you can do.

Clarissa Pinkola-Estes in **"Do Not Lose Heart"**

The Blessing Cup

Generous God, You have poured so much into our blessing cups. You have offered us many graced moments filled with wonders of your goodness. You have been bountiful in sharing your presence of unconditional love with us.

All-embracing God, you call us to share our cup of compassion with those who are searching, suffering, and sorely in need of our hospitality. You daily invite us to be in union with all those you have created and gathered to your heart.

Healing God, you know how our lives each have their share of heartaches and brokenness. You see the deepest recesses of our spirits where pain and confusion need the touch of your restoring power. Remind us often that broken hearts can be healed.

Perceptive and Insightful God, you see into the cup of our hearts. You know where the clutter lies. You invite us daily to pour out all that keeps us from being truly focused on communion with you. Again and again, you whisper to us: "Empty, pour out, let go of all that keeps you from being your true self."

Ever-present and Understanding God, you have created us as fully human persons. Our cup of life bears chips, stains, and cracks as does our own personality and life-story. You encourage us to see the stains as a way to transformation. You offer us wisdom and guidance to know when the cup needs to be washed and scrubbed, and when the stains need to be lovingly accepted.

Forgiving God, you know our weaknesses and failures. There are times when we resist what you are desiring to pour into the cup of our life. You know how we ignore or refuse to be open and receptive. Yet, you continue to believe in us. You are always waiting, ready to fill our cup with your generous love.

Gifting God, the contents of the cup are meant to refresh, nourish, and renew life. You call us to bless others with our cup of life. Stir up within us a desire to offer our gifts to those who need them.

Loving, Life-giving God, you continuously pour your transforming love into the cup of our lives. Like a spring rain falling into the open soil, so your love and ours is mixed and mingled into an energizing oneness. Your presence is the power we need to grow and to change. Your blessing of love enables us to commit ourselves to the unending process of spiritual transformation. How grateful we are! How ready to grow!

by Joyce Rupp, O.S.M. from **The Cup of Our Life**

It helps, now and then,
to step back and take the long view.
The Kingdom is not only beyond our efforts,
it is even beyond our vision.
We accomplish in a lifetime only a fraction of
the magnificent enterprise that is God's work.
Nothing that we do is complete,
which is another way of saying that the
Kingdom always lies beyond us.

No statement says all that could be said.
No prayer fully expresses our faith.
No confession brings perfection,
no pastoral visit brings wholeness.
No program accomplishes the church's mission.
No set of goals and objectives includes everything.

This is what we are about.
We plant the seeds that one day will grow.
We water the seeds already planted,
knowing that they hold future promise.
We lay foundations that will need further development.
We provide yeast that produces the effects
far beyond our capabilities.
We cannot do everything, and there is a sense
of liberation in realizing that.

This enables us to do something, and to do it well.
It may be incomplete, but it is a beginning, a step along the way,
an opportunity for the Lord's grace to enter in and do the rest.
We may never see the end results, but that is the difference
between the master builder and the worker.
We are workers, not master builders, ministers, not messiahs.
We are prophets of a future not our own.

Archbishop Oscar Romero

Christ in my mind
    that I may see what is true;

Christ in my mouth
    that I may speak with power;

Christ in my heart
    that I may learn to be touched;

Christ in my hands
    that I may work with tenderness;

Christ in my soul
    that I may know my desire;

Christ in my arms
    that I may embrace without fear;

Christ in my face
    that I may shine with God.

by Janet Morely from **All Desires Known**, expanded edition

Examen

Based on the teaching of St. Ignatius of Loyola
Adapted by Matthew and Dennis Linn, and Sheila Fabricant in their book
Sleeping with Bread: Holding What Gives You Life

WHAT: At least five minutes of daily prayer with these questions (or
variations below)
1.   For what moment today am I most grateful?
2.   For what moment today am I least grateful?

WHEN: At the end of the day.

WHO: Alone, with your journal. This can be especially effective
when shared with spouse, friends, children, special groups.

HOW: Method is simple:

1. Light a candle and do whatever you can to remind yourself of God's unconditional love for you (e.g., play a hymn, gaze upon an icon or the cross, repeats several times a mantra such as "God loves me as I am").

2. Place your hand on your heart and ask Jesus to bring to your heart a moment today for which you are most grateful. If you could relive one moment, what would it be: Where were you most able to give and receive love? What was said and done in that moment that made it so special? Breathe in the gratitude and receive life again from that moment.

3. Ask Jesus to bring to your heart that moment for which you were least grateful. When were you least able to give and receive love? What was said and done in that moment that made it so difficult? Be with whatever you feel without trying to change or fix it in any way. If comfortable, take in deep breaths and let God' love fill you as you are.

4. Give thanks for the experience and share as much as you wish with a friend.

Variations on the questions: When did I feel most alive? Most drained of life? * When was I happiest? Saddest? * When did I have the greatest sense of belonging to myself, others, God, the universe? The least sense of belonging? * What was the high point of the day? The low point? * What do I feel good about today? Where was my greatest struggle?

Present Spiritual Directors for the Samaritan Woman Directed Retreat

Consult trafford.com webpage for additional directors. This list will be updated as more spiritual directors are trained. Person coming from a great distance to make the retreat should arrange for the option of 10 days in a row. Your director will recommend affordable accommodations.

In Southern California:

Karen Basquez, Upland
909-949-7226

Sherry Clements, Simi Valley
805-526-8379

Diane Eisenman, Glendale
818-957-8813

Laura Gormley, SSL, Santa Fe Springs
562-903-0019

Sandra Linderman, Monrovia
626-205-2107

Rev. Marilyn Omernick, Los Angeles, Studio City
323-273-3888

Meg Reardon, La Cañada
818-790-2592

Judy Rinek, SNJM, Sierra Madre, Orange
626-353-6032

In Northern California:

Linda Marie Amador, Lodi
209-401-6739

In New Jersey:

Cynthia Bailey-Manns, West Orange
626-627-0726

12

Bibliography: What Gives More Depth of Understanding?

Primary Reference:

Bey-Carrión, Almita, *The Samaritan Woman Directed Retreat*, Thesis for M.A. in Spirituality, Santa Clara University, May 11, 1992. Foundation for this retreat. Quotations from a 2005 edited version of this thesis appear throughout the handbook.

Incorporated in Thesis:

- Barry, William A., S.J., Connolly, William J. S.J., *The Practice of Spiritual Direction*, The Seabury Press, 1983.
- Brennan, Anne, and Brewi, Janice, *Mid-life Directions: Praying and Playing Sources of New Dynamism*, Paulist Press, 1985.
- Brown, Raymond E., S.S., *The Gospel According to John*, Vol. 29, The Anchor Bible, Doubleday and Company, 1966.
- Bryant, Christopher, *Jung and the Christian Way*, The Seabury Press, 1983.
- Charpentier, Etienne, *How to Read the New Testament*, Crossroad, 1986.
- Cowan, Marian, C.S.J. and Futrell, John Carroll, S.J., *The Spiritual Exercises of St. Ignatius of Loyola*, LeJacq Publishing Company, 1982.
- Crossan, Dominic, O.S.M., *The Gospel of Eternal Life*, The Bruce Publishing Co., 1967.
- Ellis, Peter F., *The Genius of John*, The Liturgical Press, 1984.
- Gratton, Carolyn, *Guidelines for Spiritual Direction*, Dimension Books, 1980.
- Howes, Elizabeth Boyden, *Intersection and Beyond*, Vols. I and II, Guild for Psychological Studies Publishing House, 1971 and 1986.

- Jung, Carl G., *Collected Works*, Vol. 2, ed. Sir Herbert Read, Michael Fordham, Gerhard Adler; trans. R.F.C. Hull, Bollingen Series 20, Princeton University Press, 1985.
- Kelsey, Morton T., *Christo-Psychology*, Crossroad Publishing Company, 1982.
- *"Living the Passion of Christ"*, vol. 23, *Studies in Passionist History and Spirituality*, Passionist Generalate, 1989.
- Perkins, Pheme, *Reading the New Testament*, Paulist Press, 1977.
- Schnackenburg, Rudolf, *The Gospel According to John*, Vol. 1, Crossroad Publishing Company, 1990.
- Ulanov, Ann Belford, *Receiving Woman: Studies in the Psychology and Theology of the Feminine*, The Westminster Press, 1981.
- Vawter, Bruce, C.M., "The Gospel According to John" in *The Jerome Biblical Commentary*, Prentice-Hall, Inc., 1968.
- Wehr, Deamris, *Jung and Feminism*, Beacon Press, 1987.
- Wolff, Hanna, *Jesus the Therapist*, Meyer Stone Books, 1987.
- Youngblut, John R., *The Gentle Art of Spiritual Guidance*, Amity House, 1988.

Annotated Bibliography of Recommended Resources:

Benedictine

Casey, Michael, *Sacred Reading: The Ancient Art of Lectio Divina*, Ligouri/Triumph, 1996. Detailed guide to the Lectio; shows how it can lead to a deeper sense of presence of God and contemplation.

Freeman, Laurence, *Jesus the Teacher Within*, Continuum, 2000. Excellent reflection on the historical and risen Christ, especially coming to know him in the *Lectio Divina* meditation and contemplative prayer.

Hall, Thelma, *Too Deep for Words: Rediscovering Lectio Divina*, Paulist Press, 1988. Very practical introduction into the meditation method and 500 scripture texts that lend themselves to fruitful meditation and contemplation.

McQuiston, John, II, *Always We Begin Again: The Benedictine Way of Living*, Morehouse Publishing, 1996. The essentials of a balanced life and a contemporary interpretation of the Benedictine rule. Especially good are the sections on the first rule—listening, receptivity and thanksgiving—and the twelve stages of humility.

Dream Work

Berne, Patricia H., and Savary, Louis M., *Dream Symbol Work: Unlocking the Energy from Dreams and Spiritual Experiences*, Paulist Press, 1991. Provides a wide range of techniques to explore the meaning and insights for healing from dreams. More reference to the religious experience of Christians is found in an earlier work: Savary, Louis M., Berne, Patricia H., and Williams, Strephon Kaplan, *Dreams and Spiritual Growth: A Christian Approach to Dreamwork*, Paulist Press, 1984.

Clift, Jean Dalby and Clift, Wallace B., *Symbols of Transformation in Dreams*, The Crossroad Publishing Company, 1988. An excellent companion is working with dreams from the Jungian perspective.

Taylor, Jeremy, *Techniques for Discovering the Creative Power in Dreams*, Paulist Press, 1983. Basic manual for all aspects of dream recall, meaning, individual and group work with dreams.

Taylor, Jeremy, *Where People Fly and Water Runs Uphill: Using Dreams to Tap the Wisdom of the Unconscious*, Warner Book, 1992. Dealing with topics ranging from recurrent nightmares to connection with the Divine, Jeremy distills 20 years of working with dreams and dream groups into an excellent guide into this realm of truth, healing, wisdom and creativity.

Ignatian

Alphonso, Herbert, S.J., *The Personal Vocation: Transformation in Depth through the Spiritual Exercises*, Paulist Press, 2001. An excellent and more radical exploration of Ignatian "Election." Going beyond a mere retreat resolution, he proposes that the purpose of the Ignatian Exercises is conversion, discovery and freedom to live one's personal vocation.

Asselin, David T., S.J., "Notes on Adapting the Exercises of St. Ignatius," fom *Notes on the Spiritual Exercises of St. Ignatius of Loyola*, ed. David L. Fleming, S.J., 1983. An excellent summary of the best articles that appeared in the journal, *Review for Religious*, from 1967–1978. Contains many essentials of the Spiritual Exercises.

Bergan, Jacqueline Syrup and Schwan, Marie, *Praying with Ignatius of Loyola*, St. Mary's Press, Christian Brothers Publications, 1991. Contains a variety of meditations utilizing the spirituality and experience of St. Ignatius.

Cowan, Marian, C.S.J. and Futrell, John Carroll, S.J., *Companions in Grace: A Handbook for Directors of the Spiritual Exercises of St. Ignatius of Loyola*, Sheed and Ward, 1993. Practical reflections as the retreat progresses.

Conroy, Maureen, *The Discerning Heart: Discovering a Personal God*, Loyola University Press, 1993. Excellent primer on Ignatian Spirituality. Explores the dynamics of discernment in the lives of several types of persons.

Tetlow, S.J., Joseph, *Choosing Christ in the World: Directing the Spiritual Exercises of St. Ignatius of Loyola According to Annotations Eighteen and Nineteen: A Handbook*, The Institute of Jesuit Sources, 1989. Excellent materials for the retreatant and the director in a contemporary translation.

http://sacredspace.ie Daily prayer on the web sponsored by the Irish Jesuits that includes several resources from Ignatian spirituality for deepening the reflection and carrying it into the day.

http://www2.creighton.edu/CollaborativeMinistry/cmo-retreat.html Several prayer opportunities on the internet sponsored by the Jesuits at Creighton University, including a guided experience of the Spiritual Exercises of St. Ignatius.

Journal

Baldwin, Christina, *Life's Companion: Journal Writing as a Spiritual Quest*, Bantam Books, 1991. Recommended highly by Almita for on-going writing.

Broyles, Anne, *Journaling: a Spiritual Journey*, Upper Room Books, 1999. Looks at several jumping off places for journal writing such as scripture, dreams, daily events, conversations, quotations.

Ganim, Barbara and Fox, Susan, *Visual Journaling: Going Deeper Than Words*, Quest Books, 1999. Provides artistic and written processes for getting in touch with inner images and feelings. Dialoging with them can reduce stress, release anger, resolve conflicts and give voice to the soul.

Marqulies, Nancy, Maal, Nusa, *Mapping Inner Space: Learning and Teaching Visual Mapping*, Second Edition, Zepher Press, c. 2002. When dealing with writers block or emotional overload, a person may find mind mapping an insightful tool to clarify experience and facilitate his or her journal writing.

Morgan, Richard L., *Remembering Your Story: A Guide to Spiritual Autobiography, Revised Edition*, Upper Room Books, 2002. Using scripture and guided experiences, this book helps to become more aware of meaningful stories in life and share them.

Jungian and Psychological

Chittester, Joan, D., *Scarred by Struggle, Transformed by Hope*, William B. Eerdmans Publishing Company, 2003. With each challenge in crisis and suffering comes a gift.

Ford, Debbie, *The Dark Side of the Light Chasers: Reclaiming Your Power, Creativity, Brilliance and Dreams*, Riverhead Books, 1998. Exercises that help people embrace the elusive shadow side of their personality.

Miller, William A., *Make Friends With Your Shadow: How to Use Positively the Negative Side of Your Personality*, Augsberg, 1981. A classic in the Jungian approach to what is buried in the sub-conscious. Very helpful perspective in looking at the "well."

Moore, Thomas, *Dark Nights of the Soul: A Guide to Finding Your Way Through Life's Ordeals*, Gotham Books, 2004. Delving into the mystery of human suffering, Moore discovers the agenda of the soul is always wholeness and the abundance of life.

Myss, Caroline, "Anatomy of the Spirit: The Seven Stages of Power and Healing" audiotape, Sounds True, 1996. Fascinating illustration of psycho-spiritual growth using a synthesis of Christian sacraments, Hindu chakras, and Jewish mysticism, tree of life. The tape is very practical; she also has a book by the same name that is less anecdotal and more in depth, Harmony Books, 1996.

Pearson, Carol S., *The Hero Within: Six Archetypes We Live By* (expanded edition), HarperCollins, 1989. Insight into the myths that define who we are; exercises designed to awaken and illumine these archetypes so they can work positively toward growth.

Rohr, Richard, O.F.M., "Men and Women: the Journey of Spiritual Transformation" audiotape, St. Anthony Messenger Press, 1992. Integrates psychology and theology as he illustrates the different stages men and women go through in their maturing process.

Sofield, Loughlan, S.T., Juliano, Carroll, S.H.C.J., and Hammett, Rosine, C.S.C., *Design for Wholeness: Dealing With Anger, Learning to Forgive, Building Self-Esteem*, Ave Maria Press, 1990. Wise and practical in its approach to several areas that undermine the fullness of life. Lack of forgiveness, low self-esteem, and anger repressed as depression are common "wells."

Ulanov, Ann Bedford, *Picturing God*, Wipf and Stock Publishers, 1986. Jungian look at images and relationship with God.

Welch, John, O.Carm., *Spiritual Pilgrims: Carl Jung and Teresa of Avila*, Paulist Press, 1982. Outstanding integration of Jungian psychology and Teresa of Avila's book, *The Interior Castle*.

Wicks, Robert J., *Touching the Holy: Ordinariness, Self-Esteem, and Friendship*, Ave Maria Press, 1992. Spiritual and psychological resources in everyday life that are essential for holiness

Mandala

Cornell, Judith, PH.D., *Mandala: Luminous Symbols for Healing*, Quest Books, 1994. A practical, inspirational and beautiful guide to drawing mandalas. She guides the process of drawing with meditation and concrete directions.

Fincher, Susanne F., *Creating Mandalas for Insight, Healing and Self Expression*, Shambhala Publications, 1991. Using mandalas for therapy, she explores their origin, use and meaning. She describes all 12 stages of art therapist Joan Kellogg's theory of growth and development in the human psyche.

Fincher, Susanne F., *Coloring Mandalas for Insight, Healing and Self Expression*, Shambhala Publications, 2000. 48 designs to explore and color based on the 12th stage in Joan Kellogg's theory of growth and development in the human psyche, the Great Round.

Fincher, Susanne F., *Coloring Mandalas 2 for Balance, Harmony and Spiritual Well-being*, Shambhala Publications, 2004. 72 designs to explore and color based on the 9th stage in Joan Kellogg's theory of growth and development in the human psyche, the Crystallization. They celebrate achievements and personal creativity. This is a time when spiritual nature comes together in harmony with our physical nature.

Mid-Life Spirituality

Carroll, L. Patrick, and Dyckman, Katherine Marie, S.N.J.M., *Chaos or Creation: Spirituality in Mid-Life*, Paulist Press, 1986. Connects the several psychological and spiritual perspectives that address mid-life issues.

Estes, Clarissa Pinkola, *Women Who Run With the Wolves: Myths and Stories of the Wild Woman Archetype*, Ballantine Books, 1992. Through stories and her experience as a Jungian analyst, Clarissa Pinkola Estes addresses mid-life issues and the path to growth and creative expression, especially for women.

Kidd, Sue Monk, *When the Heart Waits: Spiritual Direction for Life's Sacred Questions*, HarperCollins, 1990. Based on the story of her own mid-life journey, Sue Monk Kidd identifies the resources and attitudes, especially that of waiting, that brought her to transformation and spiritual awakening. Image of the life cycle of the butterfly is key.

Robb, Passage *Through Mid-Life: A Spiritual Journey to Wholeness*, Ave Maria Press, 2005. Influenced by Elizabeth Kubler-Ross, the author explores the stages of dying and rising taking place in mid-life—denial, anger, anxiety, grieving, hope, suffering, acceptance and being led within.

Rupp, Joyce, O.S.M., *Dear Heart, Come Home: The Path of Midlife Spirituality*, The Crossroad Publishing Company, 1997. Guided meditations and reflections on the journey to one's full being and destiny.

Rupp, Joyce, O.S.M., *Little Pieces of Light: Darkness & Personal Growth*, Paulist Press, 1994. Illuminates the possibilities for growth in darkness, especially the questions to ask.

Mission

Covey, Stephen R., *The 8th Habit: From Effectiveness to Greatness*, Free Press, 2004. Including a DVD of film clips to illustrate his insight, Covey had re-visited his book, *The 7 Habits for Highly Effective People*, from a spiritual perspective. Excellent for coming to a sense of mission and choosing behaviors to support and enhance it.

Jones, Laurie Beth, *The Path: Creating Your Mission Statement for Work and for Life*, Hyperion, 1996. Exercises and questions that assist in articulating a person's true destiny.

Tracy, Brian, "The Psychology of Achievement," audio CD, Nightingale-Conant, 1984. Comprehensive coverage of origin of self-esteem and how to develop in a more positive way, exercises to help identify goals and mission in a way that motivates a person to accomplish them, and strategies to access ones creativity and capacity for better relationships.

Prayer

Au, Wilkie, *The Enduring Heart: Spirituality for the Long Haul*, Paulist Press, 2000. Spiritual exercises to get beyond the stuck places in life and become rooted and fruitful.

Humphreys, Carolyn, *From Ash to Fire: An Odyssey in Prayer*, New City Press, 1992. An outstanding contemporary view of the spiritual journey from Teresa of Avila's Interior Castle image.

Keating, Thomas, *Open Mind, Open Heart: The Contemplative Dimension of the Gospel*, Continuum, 1992. Basic and helpful reference in developing contemplative prayer practice.

Loder, Ted, *Guerrillas of Grace: Prayers for the Battle*, LuraMedia, 1984. A variety of poem prayers for different needs and occasions.

Rupp, Joyce, O.S.M., *The Cup of Our Life*, Ave Maria Press, 1997. Using the cup as a metaphor for different movements in the spiritual journey, Joyce provides several ways of prayer for individuals and groups. The blessing cup prayer on pp. 171–173 is a good summary of the retreat.

Rupp, Joyce, O.S.M., *Out of the Ordinary: prayers, poems and reflections for every season*, Ave Maria Press, 2000. A wide variety of prayers for appropriate occasions.

Rupp, Joyce, O.S.M., *Praying Your Goodbyes*, Ave Maria Press, 1988. Prayer and ritual related to grieving and letting go. Can get ideas there for the final ritual of the retreat.

Rupp, Joyce, O.S.M., *Prayers to Sophia*, Innisfree Press, Inc., 2000. Poetic prayers addressing Sophia, a feminine image of God.

Van Kaam, Adrian, C.S.Sp., *The Woman at the Well*, Dimension Books, 1976. Using a meditative approach, this formative scripture leads to prayer and personal application.

Wuellner, Flora Slosson, *Enter by the Gate: Jesus 7 Guidelines When Making Hard Choices*, The Upper Room, 2004. Prayer and reflections for discernment.

Wuellner, Flora Slosson, *Forgiveness, the Passionate Journey: Nine Steps of Forgiving Through Jesus' Beatitudes*, The Upper Room, 2001. Practical approach to understanding the process and power of forgiveness in life.

Wuellner, Flora Slosson, *Release: Healing from Wounds of Family, Church and Community*, The Upper Room, 1996. Guided meditations based on Scriptural images and passages for healing.

Wuellner, Flora Slosson, *Prayer, Stress, & Our Inner Wounds*, The Upper Room, 1985. A variety of practical meditations. Includes a reflection on what our wounded powers look like when transformed.

Wuellner, Flora Slosson, *Prayer and Our Bodies*, The Upper Room, 1987. A ground-breaking book on the partnership of the body, mind and spirit, on how to listen to the body as to a spiritual director.

Wuellner, Flora Slosson, *Prayer, Fear and Our Powers, Finding Our Healing Release and Growth in Christ*, The Upper Room, 1989. A look at spiritual gifts and empowerment.

Scripture

Brother of John of Taizè, *At the Wellspring: Jesus and the Samaritan Woman*, Alba House Publishing, 2001. Scriptural background and further questions that reveal the power of this story.

Brown, Raymond E., S.S., *A Retreat With John the Evangelist: That You May Have Life*, St. Anthony Messenger Press, 1998. Helpful background on John and his purposes in writing from a spirituality perspective. Day 3 on discipleship directly addresses Samaritan woman story.

Bryant, Charles V., *Rediscovering Our Spiritual Gifts*, Upper Room Books, 1991. And excellent resource on what spiritual gifts are and are not, and how to discover/realize your own spiritual gifts.

Keating, Thomas, *Fruits and Gifts of the Holy Spirit*, Lantern Books, 2000. A way to make more explicit the manifestation of the Spirit in everyday life.

McKenna, Megan, *And Morning Came: Scriptures of the Resurrection*, Sheed and Ward, 2003. Pondering the Scriptural accounts of the resurrection, Megan challenges and inspires a person to live it. Life-changing; birth, rebirth wins out over death.

McKenzie, Vashti M. *Journey to the Well*, Viking Compass Publishing, 2002. A treatment of the story in 12 meditations. It provides additional resources, meditations and journal work.

Pfeifer, Carl J., *Presences of Jesus*, Twenty Third Publications, 1984. Unique perspective on the kinds of presence in human experience, the historical Jesus, and the Risen Christ of faith.

Schneiders, Sandra M., *Written That You May Believe: Encountering Jesus in the Fourth Gospel*, The Crossroad Publishing Company, 1999. Scholarly and readable theology of John's Gospel. The role of women in the community is explored.

Spiritual Direction:

Conroy, Maureen, *Looking into the Well: Supervision of Spiritual Direction*, Loyola University Press, 1995. Good supervision tool—rationale, case studies with purpose, content, process and skills needed for a professional support and development.

Guenther, Margaret, *The Art of Spiritual Direction*, Cowley Publications, 1992. Spiritual direction from a woman's perspective—holy listening, welcoming the stranger, good teachers, midwife to the soul.

Ruffing, Janet K., *Spiritual Direction Beyond Beginnings*, Paulist Press, 2000. Several useful chapters—"Resistance in Spiritual Direction", "Love Mysticism in Spiritual Direction", "Mutuality with God", "Transference and Counter Transference in Spiritual Direction."

Silver, Anne Winchell, *Trustworthy Connections: Interpersonal Issues in Spiritual Direction*, Cowley Publications, 2003. A practical look at the spiritual direction environment, relationship and ethics.

Twelve Steps:

Alcoholics Anonymous, *The Big Book*, A.A. World Services Inc., Fourth Edition, New and Revised, 2001. A classic in exploring the spirituality and program of the Twelve Steps.

Beattie, Melody, *Codependent No More: How to Stop Controlling Others and Start Caring for Yourself*, Hazeldon, 1992. A classic in the number one tendency of women to care more for others. A classic book about the number one tendency of women to care more for others than oneself.

Kurtz, Ernest and Ketcham, Katherine, *The Spirituality of Imperfection*, Bantam Books, 1991. Very powerful insights. Here is a quote from a reader on Amazon.com: "Finding this spirituality of imperfection in Alcoholics Anonymous and twelve-step programs, K&K find the essence of the spiritual in human imperfections and failure, in the inevitability of pain. Spirituality is not the evasion of consequences or errors, but rather learning how to live with them."

May, Gerald G., *Addiction and Grace: Love and Spirituality in the Healing of Addictions*, Harper Collins, 1988. A classic exploration of the power of compulsions and addictions in most every life. A deep insight into the spiritual power of Twelve Step spirituality.

May, Gerald, G., *The Awakened Heart: Living Beyond Addiction*, Harper Collins, 1991. Grounded in the Twelve Steps, this is a guide to enter more deeply into spirituality and relationship, to move beyond the healing model into a contemplative model.

Mortz, Mary E., *Overcoming Our Compulsions: Using the Twelve Steps and the Enneagram as Spiritual Tools for Life*, Triumph Books, 1994. Very practical and resourceful ways for spiritual growth using the lenses of Twelve Steps and Enneagram.

Women's Spirituality

Ashcroft, Mary Ellen, *Spirited Women: Encountering the First Women Believers*, Augberg Fortress, 2000. Helps the Gospel come alive by creating lively dialogue and imagining more details of the story.

Dyckman, Katherine, Garvin, Mary, and Liebert, Elizabeth, *The Spiritual Exercises Reclaimed: Uncovering Liberating Possibilities for Women*, 2001. Insights into women's spiritual experience and ways of adapting the Spiritual Exercises of St. Ignatius to cultural and gender differences.

Fisher, Kathleen, *Women at the Well: Feminist Perspectives on Spiritual Direction*, Paulist Press, 1988. Useful for directing women, especially chapters "Women Experiencing and Naming God," "Jesus and Women," "Praying with Scripture," and "Women and Power".

Gateley, Edwina, *Soul Sisters: Women in Scripture Speak to Women Today*, Orbis, 2002. Poetic and artistic reflections on the story of biblical women. Captures their vision and spirit.

Printed in the United States
by Baker & Taylor Publisher Services